Our Shrinking Planet

Our Shrinking Planet

Massimo Livi Bacci

Translated by David Broder

polity

First published in Italian as *Il pianeta stretto* © Società editrice Il Mulino, Bologna, 2015

This English edition © Polity Press, 2017

Polity Press
65 Bridge Street
Cambridge CB2 1UR, UK

Polity Press
101 Station Landing
Suite 300
Medford, MA 02155
USA

ISBN-13: 978-1-5095-1583-7
ISBN-13: 978-1-5095-1584-4 (pb)

A catalogue record for this book is available from the British Library.

Typeset in 10.5 on 12 pt Sabon Roman by Toppan Best-set Premedia Limited
Printed and bound in the United Kingdom by Clays Ltd, St Ives PLC

The publisher has used its best endeavours to ensure that the URLs for external websites referred to in this book are correct and active at the time of going to press. However, the publisher has no responsibility for the websites and can make no guarantee that a site will remain live or that the content is or will remain appropriate.

Every effort has been made to trace all copyright holders, but if any have been inadvertently overlooked the publisher will be pleased to include any necessary credits in any subsequent reprint or edition.

For further information on Polity, visit our website: politybooks.com

Contents

society ♦ Rigid ages, flexible roles ♦ Four
generations under one roof

Poverty and hunger: The millennium
development goals reached ♦ But the numbers
of poor and hungry in Africa increase ♦ The
burden of 168 objectives ♦ The Malthusian
trap ♦ Nuclear-armed India with one in five
children wasted ♦ Political mission: Concentrate
efforts, dismantle the trap

A thousand times more crowded, a thousand
times smaller ♦ Still today a pendulum of fear
between overpopulation and depopulation ♦
Seven demographic and political notes ♦
Awareness of limits

Author's Note

The data cited in this book come mostly from official sources, from the United Nations to the Food and Agriculture Organization and the World Bank. More specifically, the population data from 1950 onward are drawn from the UN's *World Population Prospects: The 2015 Revision* (esa.un.org/unpd/wpp), unless otherwise indicated. The data subsequent to 2015 are drawn from the same source, on the basis of the so-called 'median variant' of UN projections (there is also a 'low' and 'high' variant). In practice, the median variant is based on reasonable, widely accepted hypotheses as to how demographic variables will develop in the future. It can be used as a genuine prediction, ignoring the UN's own semantic subtleties in distinguishing between 'prospects' and 'predictions'. In the text I have used the expressions 'developed countries', 'rich countries', and 'western countries' interchangeably, and so, too, the opposite expressions 'developing countries', 'less developed countries', and 'poor countries'. According to the UN classification, the developed countries are the countries of Europe and North America as well as Japan, Australia, and New Zealand. All the others are 'less developed countries' (even if some of them are quite developed today). In the text I often make reference to two overall indices: the mean number of children per woman; and life expectancy at birth. The former measures the average number of children born to a woman who survives through the entire fertile life cycle (and thus it overlooks mortality). Life expectancy (understood to mean life expectancy at birth, unless some other age is explicitly mentioned) represents the mean number of years lived by a newborn during her life, subject to the risks of death prevalent across all age groups at the moment of birth.

Introduction

The planet has got smaller. A thousand times smaller.

In the age of the birth of agriculture, 10,000 years ago, the 10 million human beings who populated the Earth (theoretically) had at their disposal some 13 km² of land each – an area equivalent to a quarter of the island of Manhattan per head. By 2050 there will be 10 billion of us, and the area at the disposal of each human being will be 10,000 times smaller – of the dimensions of a football pitch.

The first journey circumnavigating the world, completed by the Magellan–Elcano expedition, set off from Seville on 10 August 1519 and arrived back there on 8 September 1522, after a 1,125-day voyage. Today it takes just one day for a supersonic plane to circumnavigate the globe. It is 1,000 times faster.

The early agriculturists could draw on a few thousand calories a day: their own bodily and muscular energy, the energy provided by beasts of burden, and the energy that streams supplied to mills and the wind to sails. In our own time, an inhabitant of any of the richest countries can draw on 100 times more energy each day.

There are 1,000 times more of us, 1,000 times poorer for space; 1,000 times faster in travelling across it; 100 times greedier for energy. It should be understood that these are but crude averages in a world in which the space that people are provided with, their capacity to move around, and the energy available to them are distributed in an extremely unequal manner. But how unequal? Taking individual countries as our reference, in 2013 the GDP per capita in the richest country (Norway, at $102,700) was almost 400 times greater than that in the poorest (Burundi, at $260).

Our Shrinking Planet discusses some of the most crucial questions of our current century, linked to the Earth's population and the very powerful growth differentials across different countries, regions, and continents. Many interpret the slowdown of the planet's population growth as the sign of a coming 'end of demography', with the advent of a zero-growth world with homogeneous reproductive behaviours, universally low mortality rates, and the exhaustion of international migration. Yet never as in the present era has geodemography – a close relative of geopolitics – passed through such choppy waters. However, the population question does seem to be silently slipping off the international agenda. It is almost as if the failure of the 'demographic timebomb' to detonate (and this is how rapid population growth was irresponsibly defined half a century ago) gave us permission not to worry about the 3 or 4 billion extra people whom we will have to take in, feed, clothe, house, educate, and get working before the end of the century. And these extra people will also have a considerable impact on the environment.

We should be reassured by the fact that the international community has now adopted the principle of sustainability. This is certainly a positive thing, though this sacrosanct principle also risks changing into an acritical mantra, according to which everything must be 'sustainable' without this principle itself being given any binding definition. When we are looking at natural and physical phenomena, it is possible to define this term, however difficult that may be; but when it comes to social phenomena, it remains indistinct. The population question, for example, has been relegated to a secondary role among the forthcoming sustainable development goals that the international community is now preparing to pursue. Yet uncontrolled demographic growth in sub-Saharan Africa, the reproduction deficit in Europe and a good part of East Asia, the lack of the slightest international governance of migration, human intrusion into precarious environments, and the waste of space in ungoverned settlements all pose serious threats to sustainability.

With the arrival of the twenty-first century we can see many limits looming on the horizon. More than half of the globe has been altered by human intervention, whether directly or indirectly. Longevity continues to increase, but by any reasonable estimate lifespans cannot extend much further. In some parts of the world reproductivity has hit unprecedented historic lows, while in other regions it remains unchanged, close to the maximums that biology allows. Physical limits and barriers are being placed to block international migration flows. Even the weight of the human body will fall to its minimal limits among the billion malnourished, at the same time as it reaches its maximum among the growing ranks of the obese.

I repeatedly deal with these themes throughout this book, underlining the complex relations between population, development, and politics. The international community's guiding star must be the dismantling of the Malthusian trap that still ensnares one billion people: poverty, malnutrition, precarious survival, high fertility, high population growth rates, and thus fresh poverty. This trap was tough to crack in Malthus's time, but today, with the availability of new knowledge and greater resources, we can neutralise and dismantle it. The other goal is to strengthen the demographic quality of human capital: a well-informed freedom to choose, orient, and plan our own behaviours. That is, a well-informed freedom in sealing unions and marriages; in deciding whether to have children; in adopting means of consumption and lifestyles that favour survival; and in moving across territory.

The planet has got 1,000 times smaller. Let's be wise about how we live on it.

Florence, June 2015

1

Growing and Shrinking

- ♦ Eros, Thanatos, and the demographic balance in the ancient world
- ♦ From biological-instinctual conditions to individual choice
- ♦ The world's changeable geodemography
- ♦ Revolution and demographic transition: From 1 to 10 billion in two centuries

Men and women of the *Homo sapiens* species have not long been on this Earth: only for some 100,000 years. In the long arc of the world's biological evolution, this is a very short time indeed. Like other animal species, humans are motivated by a strong survival instinct. The concept of instinct is controversial and lends itself to various different interpretations. In more simple terms, we could define it as the constant attempt to avoid suffering and put off the unpleasant event that is death. The reproductive instinct is helpful to us in this sense, because the existence of family descent and the solidarity between parents and their offspring strengthen our capacity to survive. Children unable to take care of themselves survive thanks to parental care, just as old people unable to take care of themselves survive thanks to the care their children provide. The reproductive instinct and the survival instinct – Eros and Thanatos – have the same matrix and are both sustained and strengthened by experience: death is painful, reproduction is pleasurable. Over a very long period – centuries and millennia – these two instincts remained in a certain equilibrium, so to speak. Excessive reproduction (too many offspring) weakened parents' capacity to provide adequate care, protection, and nourishment to each child, thus making their survival more precarious, while a reproduction deficit (too few offspring) brought the extinction of the family, group, or clan. The balance between reproductivity and survival was continually shaken, and indeed tested, by conditions determined by external factors like climate, environment, diseases, and the availability of energy resources and food. These factors are not fixed: they change due to both natural forces (climate cycles, the biological evolution of diseases) and human ones (penetrating into new environments and new spaces, or producing new resources). Over time survival and reproduction fluctuated in tandem with these factors, but within rather restricted limits. Indeed, humans have proven able to elaborate an infinite number of strategies consistent with their survival instinct, as they sought to minimise and reduce the risks of dying and the suffering connected with it. For a long time – until the dawn of modernity – these strategies were of modest success to none: the historical and prehistoric evidence tells us that there were no significant variations in mortality and longevity. People died with more or less the same frequency in the Sun King's France, in Elizabethan England, or in the Venice of the doges as in the age of Augustus. The construction of complex and refined forms of society, the elaboration of philosophical thought, the evolution of scientific thought, and the fundamental discoveries of mathematics, physics, or astronomy helped little. Even where some people did manage to overcome the material dangers of poverty and hunger – as in the case of privileged groups of aristocrats, merchants, and landowners – mortality remained just as high among the poor layers of the population – serfs, commoners, and labourers. The destructive power of diseases, particularly infectious and transmissible ones, remained unabated. 'Invisible enemies' – microbes – were known to exist but could not yet be observed. They took charge of levelling out mortality among different social groups and layers. Even the instinct of reproduction remained circumscribed within rather limited boundaries: demographic and historical research has demonstrated that up to the end of the eighteenth century couples' sexual behaviour was largely if not totally lacking in deliberate regulation, being conditioned instead by biological or biology-related factors such as age, one's state of health, the frequency of sexual relations, and the length of the nursing period.

This premise helps us understand why across the history of humanity demographic growth has overall been modest and for long periods almost imperceptible. Biology and external constraints conditioned the two interdependent mechanisms of growth: survival (mortality) and reproduction (fertility). The poverty syndrome that gripped humanity – poverty in material resources and, above all, in understanding – kept mortality high. The average (mean) lifespan (or life expectancy at birth) rarely exceeded a third of a century. It was difficult to defeat the invisible enemy, the microbes that generated the most lethal diseases striking out of nowhere. Reproduction levels were kept high, not only in order to compensate for high mortality rates but also because humans had not 'discovered' how to limit the number of births – on average, no less than five or six per woman.[1] Naturally women and men discovered soon enough that the sex act led to childbirth, but they were not culturally equipped to separate the one from the other. Thus in the long term births and deaths remained in rough equilibrium, if we look past the – sometimes even violent – fluctuations generated by external factors and unpredictable shocks.

If we accept the plausible hypothesis that 10,000 years ago – in the era of the first beginnings of agriculture – the Earth counted a few million human inhabitants (let's say 10 million) and that in the era of Christ – and here we are on firmer ground – it counted 250 million, arithmetic tells us that the mean increase was around four extra individuals per 10,000 people per year. This was an imperceptible rate of increase. A higher mean rate of increase allowed the quarter-billion of year 0 to reach 1 billion in number around 1800, but there was still very little growth: around eight extra individuals per 10,000 people per year. These very modest growth rates, calculated across millennia, are abstract representations of demographic evolution that did not proceed at any uniform pace but through fluctuations and cycles, highs and lows, increases and decreases. Nonetheless, these rates do express the fundamental potential for population growth, which, in the long run, was rather modest.

We can identify with a degree of certainty some of the important phases that saw changes in the pace of population growth, for example after innovations that produced leaps forward in resource availability. First of all, the transition from a system of obtaining resources based on hunting and gathering to one based on agriculture, which made it possible to expand, regularise, and maintain food production and encouraged populations to settle, thus freeing them of the hardships and risks of nomadism. Secondly, the agricultural and industrial revolutions, which brought a strong expansion of food and energy resources from the eighteenth century onwards. Thirdly, the opening up of new spaces for settlement, as happened with the populations that came out of Africa in distant times and with the migration towards deserted or little populated regions and continents, in search of better living conditions. Not all these changes of pace produced acceleration, and others slowed or reversed population growth: for example the combined development of diseases, populations' vulnerability and immunity to them, and the emergence and spread of new diseases. Such was the case of the European plagues in the Justinian and late medieval cycles, or smallpox in the Americas.

The balance between survival and reproductivity that had lasted for millennia began to waver in the European and European-origin countries of the eighteenth century. This period saw a shattering of the syndrome of both material poverty and poverty of knowledge, which had acted as a powerful dam against demographic change, keeping both mortality and fertility at high levels. The agricultural and industrial revolutions increased the resources available to individuals, and this meant more energy, more resources in raw materials, and thus more manufactured goods and more food. Economists use the word 'development' to characterise this process, which came about in a complex manner. Scientific innovations in the biological and medical field identified the causes of the more common transmissible diseases and the ways to avoid or prevent them. Survival rates and lifespans increased. The survival instinct thus came to operate in a profoundly different context; yet, if it were possible to measure this instinct, we would probably find that its strength had still remained undimmed. Even if this instinct had been weakened, people's survival capacity increased. Some diseases were eliminated by public healthcare and others were taken care of by medicine, even among those individuals who had lost the will to live. Thus the survival instinct was no longer the dominant factor in the eternal effort to put off death and the suffering connected with it.

The reproductive instinct also ceased to be the decisive factor in generating offspring. Children's survival rates increased and couples were driven to have fewer of them, by adopting a practice they always knew of but had never – or only sporadically – practiced: voluntary birth control. The bind between sexuality and reproduction was cut. Parents were no longer the only source of investment in children; social mechanisms for providing education, healthcare, and protection made an increasing contribution.

Thus a profound revolution takes place: survival and reproduction are ever less governed by biology and the instincts connected to it. Sexuality and reproduction diverge, as do mortality and the survival instinct. What demographers have called a 'demographic transition' is set in motion: that is, a gradual decline in mortality, followed, after varying degrees of delay, by a gradual decline in fertility. This is a transition – or, better, a true and proper revolution – from a situation of rough equilibrium between mortality and fertility, both settled at high levels, to a new demographic regime, stabilised at lower levels for each. Given that demographic changes are gradual in nature, the length of this process is of the order of many decades. The decline in mortality precedes the decline in fertility, and the phase in between is marked by an accelerated population growth.

With the nineteenth century we left behind the era of conjecture on the dimensions of the planet. The age of statistics arrived, with ever more reliable figures. The planet's capacity for population growth strengthened, as numbers doubled from 1 to 2 billion between 1800 and 1927; a second doubling, to 4 billion, was completed by 1974, and a third doubling, to 8 billion, is predicted by 2023 (see Figure 1.1). The rate of increase accelerated from 0.5 per cent in the first half of the nineteenth century to 2 per cent between 1960 and 1980, before it fell to 1 per cent at the beginning of the current century. However, the planetwide data also demand further interpretation, for the average rate of population growth worldwide at any given moment is but the 'mean' of various very different situations. The demographic transition, or revolution, is driven and encouraged by development, which has occurred on widely varying geographic and temporal scales. For this reason, this revolution has unfolded with varied cadences in the different parts of the world. In some European regions it began at the outset of the nineteenth century, whereas across a vast area of sub-Saharan Africa it is still in its initial phases. The result of this great and still incomplete demographic revolution is that today there coexist across the world groups of humans shaped by very different dynamics. Some such groups are stationary or in slight decline, whereas others are growing at the greatest possible speed (over 3 per cent a year, which, if it is sustained, means a doubling of numbers in less than a quarter-century).

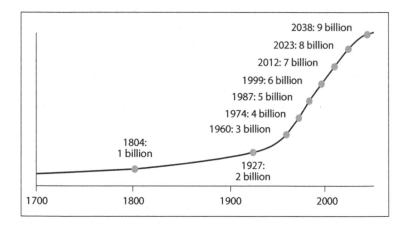

Figure 1.1 World population growth (in billions of people)
Source: United Nations, *World Population Prospects*: The 2012 Revision, New York, 2013 (at http://esa.un.org/unpd/wpp/unpp/panel_population.htm)

This is a world in the greatest of demographic 'disorder', and it is heading towards a future that is still ill defined.

Taking shape across the last two centuries, the modern world's demography bears rather little resemblance to those that characterised humanity's path across the previous hundreds and thousands of years. As we have seen, demographic mechanisms, having freed themselves from biological and instinctual ties, have acquired a growth potential enormously superior to that of the past. The gap between the long-term growth rate during the millennia that followed the discovery of agriculture and the rates reached in the 1960s is as great as the difference between the pace of the oxen pulling a cart and the speed of a jet aircraft. Yet the protagonist on this stage – humanity – is biologically the same, with invariant innate instincts and analogous faculties for reasoning. The world of the past was conditioned by a series of external constraints that compressed the capacity for population growth, just as hitting the brakes slows a vehicle's advance. With modernity, the brakes have been deactivated. However, very slow growth does not mean uniformity or lack of change. After all, even in the past there were major, geographically differentiated cycles that caused profound changes in the spatial distribution of the planet's population. Moreover, even low population-growth rates did have very important consequences in the long term. Between 1300 and 1700 the populations of Europe grew at a rather reduced speed, equivalent to around 0.2 per cent per year. Yet across this whole period the population doubled. This growth exerted powerful pressure on the systems of resource production, which in their great majority derived from agriculture or husbandry (food, wood, textiles). It was necessary to expand the areas cultivated, clear woods and forests, reclaim swampland, and use ingenuity to relaunch a stagnant productivity. The face of the continent changed considerably.

Demographic history up to 1800 offers many examples of broad cycles that changed the population structure.[2] There were powerful recessions caused by catastrophic pandemics, devastating conflicts, and profound upheavals. But there were also periods of expansion through the creation of new settlements, greater availability of resources, the attenuation or disappearance of epidemic diseases, and long periods of peace and stability. There are multiple examples of this expansion, and scholars of human population have worked to describe its development and analyse its causes. The best known and most studied cycles are those caused by pandemics. Moreover, these are often associated with other factors of turbulence and disorder, as well as with long conflicts that devastated the social and economic order and the population balance. Even a summary discussion of this subject would take up a lot of pages, so I will just run through a few paradigmatic cases.

China certainly underwent quite profound cycles. Records indicate a significant decline in population following the 1211 Mongol War of conquest. This had devastating effects – in the northern provinces more than in the southern ones – and the crisis would continue until the first part of the following century. Some estimates set the demographic decline of the thirteenth century at around a quarter of China's initial total population. An analogous demographic crisis took place after the Manchu dynasty's seizure of power in 1644, the population falling by around 10–20 million inhabitants (out of a total of 100–50 million) over the rest of the century. In the eighteenth century China entered a strong expansionary cycle, generally attributed to economic growth, the reduction of the fiscal pressure on the population, and in general an orderly and peaceable government. The population doubled from 160 to 330 million during this period. In contrast to the series of cycles in China, the nearby Indian subcontinent had a more linear demographic history.

The catastrophic effects that the conquest and the encounter with Europe had for the Americas are well known in their general outline. However, the causes of this catastrophe and indeed its dimensions remain uncertain, given the lack of documentation as well as the effect of ideological prejudices. Well-reputed scholars have offered incompatible estimates of the population decline that took place in the sixteenth century and in the first part of the seventeenth century, according to which the population is reduced by something ranging between one third and over 90 per cent, by comparison to what it had been upon first contact. The new Eurasian diseases (smallpox and other viral illnesses) that the Europeans introduced among the autochthonous populations played a leading role in this process, since these populations had not developed the relevant immunities. But equally important were the profound effects of the destabilisation that the conquest provoked. Only at the end of the seventeenth century would indigenous population levels begin to recover.

The great sub-Saharan region has precious few historical sources, facts, and data regarding demography. Development in the most populous part of the continent – the West, stretching from Mauritania to Angola – seems to have reached a halt in the eighteenth century, if not a recession, as the forcible extraction of young men and women by a greatly flourishing slave trade reached its most intensive levels. Across the century, around 5 million slaves were deported to America and an unknown – but very considerable – number were sent on the Arab trade routes, towards the North and East. This traumatic draining of reproductive-age youth, removed from a population estimated at something between 25 and 30 million, certainly had a depressive effect on growth.

Finally, a note on Europe will complete this tour of the four continents (the fifth, Oceania, remained of irrelevant demographic dimensions up until the nineteenth century). The phases of recession were linked to the first and second plague pandemics and, for Northern and Central Europe, to the Thirty Years' War (1618–48). The so-called 'plague of Justinian' – which broke out in Byzantium in 543 but continued into subsequent centuries – aggravated a negative cycle that had begun in the final phase of the Roman Empire. The plague that broke out in 1347 ['the Black Death'] raged in recursive waves until the middle of the fifteenth century, and the continent lost around a third of its population. The Thirty Years' War had similarly devastating effects in Northern and Central Europe through losses due to military events, the destruction of productive activities, and the spread of epidemics. But there were also relatively sustained expansive phases (within the limits of past populations' modest growth capacities). These phases were linked to the flourishing of urban economies and agriculture in the twelfth and thirteenth centuries and to the strong recovery after the depression that the second plague pandemic had provoked.

Given that the phases of expansion and depression in the various parts of the world were not synchronised across continents and regions, geodemography was also subject to powerful temporal variations. For example, China and India had roughly similar populations in 1700, but by 1800 the former had 1.5 times more inhabitants than the latter, thanks to the strong development I mentioned a little earlier. In the eighteenth century Japan had a stagnant population, which represented a fifth of China's population in 1700 but less than a tenth of it in 1800. Already at the moment of its conquest, the American continent held less than one tenth of the world population, but by 1700 this proportion had fallen to just 2 to 3 per cent of the total. The population of New Spain (Mexico) in 1500 was certainly much greater than that of Spain, which was conquering it at the time; but in 1700, after two centuries of colonisation, it counted for less than half.[3]

I can recap what has been said by putting it as follows. In the long term, the growth potential of premodern populations was modest, and yet these populations were nonetheless the protagonists of more or less sustained cycles of expansion and contraction. Produced by a multiplicity of factors, these cycles were not in synchrony across the various groups of humans, empires, nations, or other, lesser aggregations. Rather, they translated into powerful mutations in the world's geopolitics and geodemography.

With the end of the old demographic regime 200 years ago, the pace of change made a great forward stride. Demographic behaviours were no longer rigidly conditioned by biology – the survival instinct or the instinct for reproduction. Innovation loosened the binds of traditional external constraints and the individuals' ability to choose – namely when and how to seal a stable union, how many children to bring into the world (and when), how and when to move, and how to avoid diseases rather than simply be besieged by them – was strengthened. These are the forces driving the modern demographic transition or revolution. While it is always the same mechanism that accomplishes this process, its timing varies in terms of beginning, duration, and the gap between the initial period (marked by a decline in mortality) and the onset of the decline in birth rates.

The most aggregated level of explanation identifies the first motor for change in the decline in mortality that began in the second half of the eighteenth century. This decline was due partly to exogenous factors – the decreased importance of epidemic cycles, the plague's disappearance from Europe – partly to the lower incidence of famine on account of better economic organisation, and partly to social and cultural practices that contributed to halting the spread of infectious diseases and to improving the conditions for survival, especially in early infancy. At an aggregate level, the lowering of mortality served to accelerate growth and, as a result of the greater pressure on resources, stimulated the rebalancing mechanisms that pushed down birth rates, whether through delayed marriage or through the spread of voluntary birth control. A new balance was achieved only at the end of the process of declining fertility, which is more or less rapid depending on the various populations' differing degrees of progress. This is an adaptation of the Malthusian model, according to which the population adjusts to resources also through restrictions on growth, which are determined by a birth rate increasingly decoupled from biology and subjected to individual control (a development unforeseen by Malthus).[4]

In analysing the transition process, more disaggregated explanations privilege the change in couples' choices that was induced through the social transformation set in motion by the Industrial Revolution. In particular, the rise of an industrial and urban society causes an increase in the relative 'cost' of raising children, who become income producers – and thus autonomous – at a much later age than they do in agricultural societies. Moreover, they require greater 'investments' in terms of health, education, and welfare and also block off opportunities for work – particularly for the mother. The increase in the relative cost of children is thus held to be the incentive to restricting reproduction. According to this explanation, the action of this incentive was encouraged by the decrease in social control exercised by tradition, institutions, and religion and occurred in parallel with the process of European societies' economic and social development. This explanation also holds that there were dissemination mechanisms that facilitated the phenomenon's spread from towns to the countryside, from the more cultured and wealthy layers to the less fortunate, and from the geographic areas at the epicentre of development to peripheral regions.

The paradigm illustrated above offers a useful synthesis of the rise and spread of the demographic revolution in western countries over the course of the nineteenth century. Once the relevant adjustments are made, it can also be applied to what has happened in poorer parts of the world since the middle of the twentieth century. Figure 1.2 outlines two models: one for the western countries, whose transitions began early, in the first half of the nineteenth century, and the other for the poor countries, whose more belated transitions began around the middle of the twentieth century. The first model is spread across a very long time span, the decline in mortality is slow (it takes place in an era in which biomedicine was making gradual, even if fundamentally important progress), the gap

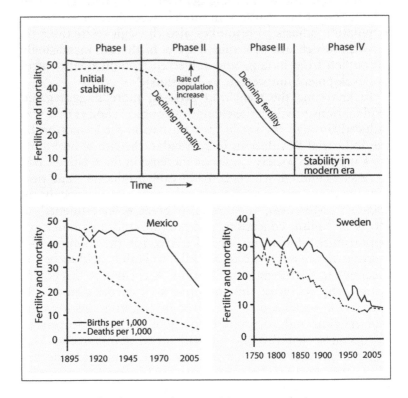

Figure 1.2   The demographic transition or revolution
Source: http://www.trunity.net/sam2/view/article/177749

between the curves of mortality and fertility is relatively contained, and the rate of increase (the gap between the two curves) does not exceede 1.5 per cent even at its peak. Conversely, the model for poor countries plays out across a shorter period, the decline in mortality is more rapid, and the rate of increase peaks at over 3 per cent. In general, between the beginning and the end of the transition, the population-growth rate is higher in the second case than in the first. Figure 1.2 presents the specific examples of Sweden and Mexico, which resemble these two model curves: during the transition Sweden's population doubles, whereas Mexico's increases five times.

Table 1.1 provides a synthesis of demographic developments over the past two centuries, reported according to large continental areas, including China and India. From it we can clearly make out the slowdown in demographic growth in Europe and North America over the last century by

Table 1.1 Population of the continents, China, and India in 1820, 1913, and 2020

	Population (in millions)			Annual increase per 1,000	
	1820	1913	2020	1820–1913	1913–2020
Europe	224	496	740	8.5	3.8
North America	11	108	371	24.6	11.7
Central and South America	22	81	667	14.0	19.6
Asia	710	977	4,598	3.4	14.4
Africa	74	125	1,340	5.6	22.0
Oceania	1	6	42	19.3	18.2
China	381	437	1,403	1.5	11.1
India	209	304	1.389	4.0	14.0
World	1,042	1,793	7,758	5.8	13.6

Source: Angus Maddison, *World Economy: Historical Statistics*, Paris, 2020 [2003]; United Nations, *World Population Prospects: The 2012 Revision*. New York, 2013 (at http://esa.un.org/unpd/wpp/unpp/panel_population.htm)

comparison to the nineteenth and, conversely, the very powerful acceleration of demographic growth in Asia and Africa.

The main parameters of the demographic transition can be summarised as follows: the periods in which the transition begins and ends (here its final phase is arbitrarily fixed at the date where the mean number of children per woman reaches 2.5 and life expectancy reaches 70); and the maximum rate of increase reached during the transition (see Table 1.2).[5]

The beginning of Europe's transition can be situated in the first half of the nineteenth century, and that of Africa's at the end of the twentieth century. The end of the transition can be dated to the 1960s for the developed world, and for Africa (if predictions are accurate) some time in the second half of the twenty-first century. Annual growth rates peaked at 1.2 per cent in Europe and at 2.8 per cent in Africa and, whereas in the rich countries the transition lasted for over a century, in Africa as in other poor countries it lasted under one century.

This first chapter has sought to describe the demographic forces at work across the long course of human history up until our present day. But these forces have an inertial element that allows us to think about the future. This is precisely what I will do here, employing the regularly reviewed and updated projections elaborated by the United Nations. These projections make use of rigorous scientific analyses and of a 'consensus' among experts and scholars regarding the tendencies that various demographic phenomena may conceivably display across the coming century (see Author's Note). Two considerations are essential in this regard. The first is that, although these tendencies are notable for being stable over time, as the arc of the projection is extended (in our case, until the end of the century, which means a timespan of around three generations), the results contain an increasing degree of uncertainty. The second is that, while past projections (and the United Nations has been engaged in such projections for half a century) did prove fairly accurate for the world population taken as an aggregate, they increasingly presented deviations (on the side of excess or deficit) as they descended from the planetary scale to the more detailed level of continental, regional, subregional, or national areas. At the 'world' level, forecasts have it that a population estimated at close to 7.3 billion in 2015 will grow to 9.7 billion by 2050

Table 1.2 Parameters of demographic transition across the continents, China, and India

		Parameters of Transition		
	Beginning of transition	Average 2.5 children/women	Life expectancy around the age of 70	Maximum population increase
Europe	1800–50	1960–5	1965–70	1.2% (1850–1900)
North America	1800–50	1965–70	1960–5	1.8% (1960–5)
Central and South America	1920–50	2000–5	1995–2000	2.77% (1960–5)
Asia	mid-1900s	1995–2000	2005–10	2.47% (1965–70)
Africa	late 1900s	**2075–80**	**2045–50**	2.8% (1980–5)
Oceania	1850–1900	1985–90	1980–5	2.2% (1950–5)
China	mid-1900s	1990–5	1990–5	2.8% (1965–70)
India	1950–60	2010–15	**2020–5**	2.33% (1975–80)
World		2010–15	2010–15	2.07% (1960–5)

Source: United Nations, *World Population Prospects: The 2012 Revision.* New York, 2013 (at http://esa.un.org/unpd/wpp/unpp/panel_population.htm)
Note: Bold represents the author's extrapolations.

and to 11.2 billion by 2100 (3.9 billion more than today). It is difficult to evaluate how reliable such figures are, but another probabilistic study by the United Nations suggests an almost 80 per cent chance of the world population in 2100 standing at between 9.7 and 12.5 billion (which means an increase of between 2.4 and 5.2 billion by comparison to the figures of today). Let's settle for pointing our telescope at a moment rather closer in the future: 2050, around a generation from now. The level of doubt is much lower here, and we can assume with some certainty that the world population will increase by something between 2 billion and 2.5 billion over the course of the next thirty-five years. The level of increase will be determined both by a further reduction in birth rates – from 2.5 children per woman today to 2.2 in 2050 (the result of a slight recovery in wealthy countries with low birth rates and of a further diminution in poor countries) – and by the continued lengthening of life expectancy – from 71 to 77 years of age. This will mean feeding well over 2 billion 'extra' people, and also clothing and housing them; they will need fuel and energy for cooking, heating, and moving around; they will take up the raw materials for stocking themselves with essential consumer goods and work tools; and they will need space to live. This population increase also ought to be considered in terms of its territorial articulations, which can be summarised as follows:

- Almost all the future increase (98 per cent) will take place in developing countries, since forecasts tell us that in the developed countries the population will remain almost stationary.
- Over half of the population increase in the next thirty-five years will be concentrated in sub-Saharan Africa (which will double in numbers) and around 28 per cent in the Indian subcontinent.
- In the developing countries themselves, the population will increase more rapidly in extremely poor areas – where it will double – than in other, less poor ones, where it will grow by around a quarter.
- Long before 2050, the populations of Europe, China, and Japan will already have embarked upon a downward trend.

- The population in urban areas will increase rapidly, while the population in rural areas will continue to fall.
- Even if there are no specific forecasts about this, the population of coastal belts – which are more fragile and more densely populated – will increase much more quickly than that of inland areas.

However, the African demographic question is undoubtedly the most acute. The population of the sub-Saharan region will multiply by a factor of 2.2 in the next thirty-five years (from 962 million to 2.123 billion). Birth rates are on a mild downward trend: they currently amount to about 5.1 children per woman, and it is believed that they may reduce to 3.1 by 2050, as this fall accelerates. Yet if – contrary to expectations – they remain at the present levels, the population will triple by the middle of the century. Trends in birth rates over the coming decades will determine whether the region will have hundreds of millions of people over or under what is currently expected. Thus there is wide room for intervention through social policies directed at orienting – without coercion – how reproduction develops.[6]

Let's recap: over the next thirty-five years the world population will increase by almost one third, but the territorial articulations of this increase will be highly differentiated. There will be no population increase in the rich countries; a rise of around one quarter in the relatively less poor developing countries; and a doubling of numbers in the poorest countries.

I have hypothesised that 10,000 years ago, at the beginning of the Neolithic period, the world population was of the order of 10 million inhabitants. At the end of this century it will be around 1,000 times greater than that. Balancing the numbers, we see that nine tenths of this growth will have accrued in the three centuries between 1800 and 2100, and half of it in the fifty years between 1965 and 2015. This dizzying rise has upended the old balance built up over the previous millennia in mainly agricultural societies. In the following chapters I will discuss the environment, adaptability, sustainability, geopolitics, globalisation, inequalities, mobility, migration … that is to say, the mutually influential factors that intersect with the demographic tendencies I have already summarised. Up to this point I have spoken of measures of population growth, counting individual humans as if we could straightforwardly compare them over time, just as a zoologist would when counting the various species of mammals or birds in a determinate ecological belt. But humans have profoundly changed – if not in their biological traits, then certainly in their behaviours. The world in which they live – their social and ecological micro-habitats – has also changed, and this in turn conditions human behaviours. We therefore need to adjust our analytical tools so as to understand future population developments better.

As we discussed at the outset, the enormous novelty of reproductive behaviours and human survival by comparison to those of the past derives from the dissociation of biology and instinct from individual behaviours. This dissociation is connected to our increased ability to make choices regarding either reproduction or (at least in part) survival. We can choose partners, how many children to have and when, the form of a union or the family unit, and how long it should last. As concerns survival, we can choose our lifestyles and our diets; we can make use of the most appropriate physiological and medical treatments; in some jurisdictions we can even choose the means by which our lives would end. We can, moreover, choose where and when we move and make our homes (at least within the limits of a national territory). Our capacities to make such choices are not absolute (for instance, they are conditioned by economic resources). Albeit less than in our own time, humans have always been able to make such choices. Yet today these capacities have increased enormously and represent the cornerstones of human capital. Naturally, there is still much ground left to cover. We need only think of the fact that across vast swathes of the world voluntary birth control is still not widespread, and in these same regions survival remains precarious. Even so, enormous change has already been achieved, and humanity has greater capacity today than in the past to 'steer' its own trajectory. But now it also bears the responsibility of deciding 'how' to steer it and where.

2

Land, Water, Air

- ♦ Simeon Stylites and his environmental footprint
- ♦ The cabal of the $10 \times 2 \times 7$
- ♦ More than half the planet changed by human intervention
- ♦ Population and fragile regions: Coasts, forests, and urbanisation
- ♦ From the London smog of the seventeenth century to the greenhouse effect in the twenty-first

Legend has it that the ascetic penitent Simeon Stylites lived atop a pillar for thirty-seven years, only eating the minimum necessary to survive. This holy man should be raised up as a symbol and model of the most extreme environmentalism – the individual with the lightest environmental footprint in history. After all, he had almost no need for space and consumed near-imperceptible amounts. But humanity is not like Simeon. From its origins until recent times, it lived in an abundance of space, without worrying that this was a finite resource. Certainly history offers countless examples of struggles and conflicts for monopolising the best land. Once that terrain was occupied, it became necessary to make the troublesome effort to settle on less bountiful lands – by means of forest clearing, ploughing, draining, and even reclaiming land from lakes and seas. But there was an abundance of land in Africa, America, vast regions of Asia, and the very recently discovered Australasian world. This land could take in growing populations, small or large groups of migrants, or even entire nations. The Earth was expansive and without limit. Naturally here I am simplifying some very complex realities. But this is useful for the simple purpose of understanding the jump that has taken place over time – and particularly in the last two centuries – in humans' perception of the world's limits. Where yesterday these limits were remote and invisible, today they bear down on us from close proximity.

Let me give a simple example of humanity's growing 'weight' on our planet. In the two centuries from 1800 on, the Earth's population grew sevenfold, from 1 to 7 billion. But each individual today lives twice as long as in 1800 and has at his/her disposal an income ten times greater than s/he would have had back then (in real, not in monetary terms). Income is a discrete indicator of the non-renewable resources and energy consumed by each individual, and thus of that individual's potential 'impact' – which is not necessarily negative – on the environment. For the average individual, this potential impact has increased tenfold over the past two centuries. But, if we take into account the fact that s/he treads the Earth for twice as long and that in this same interval of time the population has multiplied by seven, it follows that humanity's potential impact on the planet today is 140 times $(10 \times 2 \times 7)^1$ greater than at the beginning of the nineteenth century! Naturally this figure is only for illustrative purposes and based on the most simplistic of calculations. But it gives some idea of the distance separating yesteryear's preindustrial world from today's postindustrial one, as well as of the fact that the world's physical boundaries – back then invisible and unknown – are today coming clearly into view, close on our horizon. Of course, this 'potential' can have both negative effects (the destruction of the ecosystem, contamination, wasting space) and positive ones (useful, beautiful, and efficient buildings; works to prevent destructive erosion; deserts transformed into land that can be cultivated). So this does not mean passing negative judgement – in terms of the planet's future – on the fact that an industrious humanity has become richer and more numerous. This is just a neutral recognition of the facts.

A population needs space to live. Space for housing, for food production, for community activities, for raising animals, for extracting fuel, for infrastructure. Population growth moves in tandem with the increased demand for space – space that is taken away from the natural environment. This dynamic process of anthropisation depends on a number of variables, the most powerful of which is demographic dynamics.

Let's take the case of Europe. As almost anywhere across the world, up until the Industrial Revolution its main source of nutrition was cereal products. It has been estimated that feeding a person required around 300 kg of grain per year[2] and that around 1800 it took an average of around half a hectare of land to produce this much, given the low productivity of the era's agricultural system. At the beginning of the nineteenth century, Europe's population of around 150 million people (not including Russia) thus required around 750,000 km² of land (out of a territory of around 5 million km²) to satisfy its basic food needs. Since Europe did not live on bread alone (or just on grain), it needed still further land for growing complementary foods, for grazing livestock, and for the wood necessary for heating. Add to this the space taken up by urban areas, by manufacturing activities, and by the infrastructure – however modest – of the time, and we will not be far off the truth if we conclude that anthropogenic activities took at least one third of the total space away from the natural environment. If we then take into account that another part of Europe's territory was closed off to human activities for natural reasons (freezing climates, mountainous areas, and bodies and courses of water), we can conclude that the Europeans of two centuries ago were beginning to get a clear sense of their continent's physical limits. Certainly the great transoceanic migration that began in the middle of the nineteenth century was by no means unrelated to this perception. Indeed, in many areas of Europe this lack of space was turning into an acute lack of resources, driving an intense flow of people out of the continent. Recent integrated estimates give us an approximate picture of the spread of cultivated land across the various regions of the world. Moreover,

Table 2.1 Land area cultivated per capita

	1700	1800	1900	1990
Western Europe	0.453	0.464	0.307	0.242
Eastern Europe	0.757	0.813	0.512	0.392
World	0.439	0.412	0.500	0.278

Source: K. Goldewijk, 'Estimating Global Land Use Change over the Past 300 Years: The HYDE Database', *Global Biogeochemical Cycles*, 15.2 (2001): 430

they allow us to calculate the area cultivated per capita from 1700 to our own time. Table 2.1 relates the figures in hectares for Western Europe, Eastern Europe (without Russia), and the world as a whole.

Thanks to the general improvement of productivity, the average amount of land cultivated in order to feed one person has decreased over time. The effect is that over the past three centuries the total cultivated area has increased less than the population has; in the time that the former increased fivefold, the population grew 9.5 times over. The last few decades have seen a rapid decrease in the per capita arable land area, which balances out the consequences of population growth. At the present moment the area devoted to cultivation represents around 11 per cent of the Earth's land surface; a further 31 per cent is covered by woods and forests, 15 per cent by steppes, savannah, scrubland, and brush; 20 per cent by deserts in extreme climate and by tundra; and 23 per cent by pastureland.

Table 2.2 illustrates how the distribution by use of the Earth's 134 million km² of land area changed between the undisturbed state (without human intervention) and three dates staggered between 1700 and 1990. Woods and forests, steppes and savannahs – but also, to a lesser degree, areas unsuitable for cultivation, such as tundra and deserts – have lost ground. These areas are given over to crops and, most importantly, have become pastureland necessary for sustaining a humanity whose numbers and economic means continue to increase. Cultivation and grazing are thus the subjects of a direct or indirect transforming activity (and pastureland is also expanding on account of increasing

Table 2.2   Distribution by use of Earth's land area (million km²)

	Woodland/ forests	Steppe/ savannah/ grassland	Tundra/ desert	Cropland	Pasture
Undisturbed	58.6	44.1	31.4	0.0	0.0
1700	54.4	40.8	31.1	2.7	5.2
1850	50.0	35.5	30.4	5.4	12.8
1990	41.5	20.0	26.9	14.7	31.0

Source: K. Goldewijk and N. Ramankutty, 'Land Use Changes during the Past 300 Years', in *Encyclopedia of Life Support Systems* (EOLSS), vol. 1, Unesco: Paris, 2005

per capita meat consumption). Today (or, to be exact, in 1990) the two take up little less than a half the Earth's land area.

I can complete this historical picture with a more detailed and more up-to-date look at the accounts for land use, most importantly as concerns anthropogenic interventions. One recent study[3] refers to the year 2007 and makes use of data that are becoming increasingly precise thanks to high-definition satellite imaging. The study estimates that agricultural and forest cultivation covers some 47 per cent of the Earth's land area. About 13 per cent of this sum consists of land devoted to arable use and permanent cultivation; 26 per cent is covered by permanent pastureland and meadows; and another 8 per cent is made up of areas subjected to deforestation or artificially replanted. But to this 47 per cent we also need to add the other spaces in which human action is radically changing the face of the land: 3 per cent of the land surface devoted to urban areas, another 3 per cent devoted to various types of economic activity, and a further percentage point devoted to infrastructure (roads, ports, railways) and mining activities. The total area directly used or transformed by human activity thus accounts for more than a half of the Earth's land area (54 per cent). As for the remaining 'natural' areas, 28 per cent of the total land is covered by woods and forests, while 19 per cent cannot be turned over to agriculture or other human uses because it is frozen, deserted, or situated in the mountains. (But these areas are not entirely natural

since they, too, may be affected by human activities, through
contamination or global warming.)

It is known that the growth and spread of a rapidly expanding world population's settlements presents other aspects that
may bring about challenges. Three of these aspects are particularly worth mentioning because they are linked to delicate
environmental questions that may become critically important in the coming half-century – a period in which the speed
of population growth will still be rather considerable. These
aspects are human intrusion into the great forests, and particularly into the rainforests, whose integrity is a guarantee
of the bionatural equilibrium; the intensification of human
settlement in the most precarious habitats, in particular along
coasts and along the banks of rivers and lakes; and the explosion of urbanisation processes.

Since time immemorial, human activity has caused the
gradual reduction of the natural forests that coat the Earth,
changing their characteristics. Deforestation processes have
accompanied demographic growth ever since the initial
spread of agriculture. In the past millennium, until the Industrial Revolution, Europe underwent an intense deforestation
process that closely corresponded to its population growth.
The latter was a rapid process in the 300 years before the
great plague of the fourteenth century, followed by stasis as
the population diminished after the pandemic, and then by
recovery in the following centuries. At the beginning of the
twentieth century, Europe, with the exception of its northern
part, had lost much of its original blanket of woodland, much
as the Maghreb and a good part of the Middle East had. As
for the United States, the original blanket of woodland that
still covered the country to the east of Mississippi River in
the mid-nineteenth century, from Canada to the Gulf of
Mexico, had disappeared by 1920, swept away by industrialisation and population growth. The Atlantic Forest (*Mata
Atlântica* in Portuguese), which covered Brazil's coastal belt,
had already disappeared in large part by the beginning of the
nineteenth century, having been destroyed by the felling of
valuable trees and extraction of the timber necessary for
mining activities and sugar-cane plantations. From the mid-
nineteenth century onwards India's vast blanket of forest also
came under attack, as the British Empire sought wood not

only for its shipyards and its navy but also for the construction of a very extensive rail network and for meeting the demand for fuel that the latter generated.

The deforestation of the Amazon basin is perhaps the phenomenon that arouses the greatest amount of concern and debate. It is estimated that deforestation has eaten away between 15 and 20 per cent of the blanket of rainforest. This has been the case especially since the 1940s, and the phenomenon has numerous causes: the acquisition of land for herding livestock and growing crops, driven by demand from an expanding population, as well as by international demand, timber production; mining and oil prospecting; infrastructure works; and immigration. The connection with international trade deserves underlining. China has enormously increased its imports of soy, a staple food for pigs raised in their millions, and this has led Brazilian farmers to raise their production, in part by converting strips of forest into land on which they can grow crops. In Brazilian Amazonia (so-called 'classic' Amazonia – 3.6 million km^2) the deforested area rose from 2 per cent in 1980 to 12 per cent in 2010, while in this same period the population increased 2.5 times (from 5.9 to 14.8 million) due to very heavy immigration.[4] In more recent years the government's rather more attentive policy has succeeded in putting the brakes on deforestation, which proceeded at its fastest pace around the turn of the millennium.

Similar phenomena have taken place – or are taking place – in other parts of the world. The forests of the Congo Basin cover an area of 2 million km^2; in this they are second only to the forests of the Amazon. They are seriously under threat, also because of the political instability in the region. The latest satellite imaging shows a slowdown in the pace of deforestation: for, while in the 1990s deforestation led to the destruction of 3,000 km^2, in the first decade of the new century it was reduced by one third. Even so, with a population-growth rate of over 2 per cent per year, demographic pressure will continue to be very high in coming decades, as well as the intrusions for commercial and mining exploitation. One can advance similar considerations about other vast territories covered by forests, in the Indonesian archipelago or in Papua New Guinea. The world's biggest palm oil producer, Indonesia, has seriously eaten away at the blanket of

rainforest in order to make way for industrial palm plantations. Human settlements, a growing population's demand
for foodstuffs of mass consumption, and the exploitation of
resources for manufacturing and energy industries exercise a
pressure that only robust institutions and effective norms
would be able to fight back against. Again, international
trade plays a powerful role here, and not only in terms of
minerals and oil: China and Japan both import timber from
Indonesia and Papua New Guinea.

The great forests play a crucial role in maintaining environmental balances: in moderating greenhouse gas emissions
and thus global warming; in maintaining the integrity of
water reserves; and in protecting biodiversity. But the central
problem for administrators is that trees give more (immediate) profit when they are cut down than when they are hale
and hearty and that pastureland and arable land have more
(immediate) value than virgin forests do.

The rapidly growing population of the last century has
tended to concentrate in coastal belts, which are advantageous not only in terms of their climate and landscape but
also with regard to communications and the multiplicity of
economic opportunities they offer. History teaches us that the
majority of the world's great cities rise up beside the sea or
major watercourses. But coastal cities are also the most precarious. An uncontrolled expansion of residential and industrial installations and infrastructure in such contexts has
negative effects in terms of water contamination, the changes
they bring to areas of environmental value, and exposure to
natural risks (just think of the more than 200,000 deaths
caused by the 2004 tsunami). These risks are destined to
grow, as a consequence of global warming. Coastal areas'
environmental vulnerability has become obvious in recent
years, given the recurrence of natural disasters (typhoons and
flooding by tidal surge) that strike the river delta regions of
South and South-East Asia, especially in Bangladesh.

There are not many data, and not too precise, on the distribution of population in coastal areas. First of all, there are
no standardised (and thus comparable) definitions of what
'coastal areas' actually are: there are measures such as estimating the population inhabiting a coastal belt of determinate width (10, 20 ... 100 kilometres from the sea), or,

equally crudely, counting the population in the administrative units that border the sea. For example, in Italy the coastal *comuni* washed by the sea occupy 14 per cent of the country's land area but concentrate some 28 per cent of its population: their population density amounts to 387 inhabitants per km², double the average density (197) and more than double the density of non-coastal Italy (166). In the United States, the population density in coastal counties (116 inhabitants per km²) is three times the national average (38).

Rather more precise is a recent study making use of satellite measurements, which estimates the population living within 100 kilometres of the sea but in areas at less than 10 metres above sea level in each country.[5] These are the most precarious of territories, and they are placed at further risk by rising sea levels and by the intensification of extraordinary atmospheric events. Table 2.3 reports the distribution of these areas across the continents and their relative populations. In 2000, 10 per cent of the world's population lived in

Table 2.3 Population in low-elevation coastal zones, by region and continent (2000)

	Population		Area	
	Millions	World percentage	Thousands of km²	World percentage
Africa	56	7	191	1
Asia	466	13	881	3
Europe	50	7	490	2
Latin America	29	6	397	2
Australia and New Zealand	3	13	131	2
North America	24	8	553	3
Small island states	6	13	58	16
World	634	100	2,700	2

Source: G. McGranahan, D. Balk, and B. Anderson, 'The Rising Tide: Assessing the Risks of Climate Change and Human Settlements in Low Elevation Coastal Zones', *Environment & Urbanization*, 19.1 (2007): 17–37. Copyright © 2007 by the International Institute for Environmental Development (IIED). Reprinted by permission of SAGE publications, Ltd.

low-altitude coastal regions, which constituted 2 per cent of the planet's total land area. Sixty per cent of these 634 million people lived in urban areas. In general, populations in coastal regions tend to increase more quickly than inland ones, and thus the degree of concentration along coastlines tends to increase. The same study from which I draw these aggregate data also compared the dynamics of two countries – China and Bangladesh – between 1990 and 2000. Around one third of all inhabitants of low-lying coastal areas worldwide live in these two countries. In China, over that decade, the growth rate in these areas was 1.9 per cent, as against 1 per cent nationwide; in Bangladesh the respective growth rates were 2.1 per cent and 1.1 per cent.[6]

According to United Nations estimates, the world's urban population has now surpassed the world's rural population: already in 2014 town and city dwellers made up 53 per cent of the total, and this proportion is destined to increase in the coming decades. In many developed countries the population classified as 'urban' is more than 80 per cent of the total. Two or three centuries ago the opposite was the case: it has been calculated that in Europe in 1800 the population living in urban centres with more than 10,000 inhabitants accounted for around 10 per cent of the continent's total. These towns and cities took up a very modest share of the overall land area: they were often surrounded by walls and densely settled. But we should also pay attention to the fact that the inhabitants had to avail themselves of food supplies, fuel, and other provisions and thus had an impact on a territory far wider than the one delimited by the city walls.[7] Stacking up the numbers for purely illustrative purposes – as I did above – one could calculate that 10,000 inhabitants of a hypothetical city could be fed on 3,000,000 kg of grain (300 kg per head per year, if cereals were their only nourishment) and that, given the productivity of the time, this amount of grain could have been harvested from a seeded area of 30 km². Apart from food, the city's residents also needed wood supplies for cooking, heating, and other uses, at a consumption rate estimated at around 1 tonne per person per year. The total of 10,000 tonnes could have been provided by a well-managed area of woodland of 50 km². If one adds other resources procured from outside the city walls (animal and vegetable fibres, produce from grazing livestock), supporting our hypothetical city would have required the use of an area (arable land, woodland, and pastureland) of around 100 km². Therefore its environmental footprint would have made its mark on a very wide area. And then a network of cities would have sought interconnection through roads and bridges, man-made waterways and ports. Two hundred years ago this type of urban structure was probably in a good balance with the landscape and the environment.

Yet everywhere development has wiped away this type of urbanisation

Today a growing proportion of the population classified as urban lives in big and sprawling conurbations with ill-defined boundaries. In 1950 there were two so-called 'megacities' or conglomerates of over 10 million inhabitants; by 1990 there were ten of them, and by 2014 there were twenty-eight. Meanwhile big cities of 5 to 10 million inhabitants, of which there were twenty-one in 1991, more than doubled to forty-three in 2014, while the number of small cities – cities of 1 to 5 million people, small only according to international terminology – rose from 239 to 4,158. Demographic concentration in urban areas is not by itself a negative phenomenon. Humans are essentially gregarious animals and tend to live in restricted spaces. But the modern mega-urbanisation process has been compressed into a very short period of time, in a disorderly and often anarchic way. Its negative consequences for the environment relate above all to air pollution – with its well-known ill effects for health – and water contamination, with effects that spread out into the ecosystem well beyond the megacity's own territory. All that, as well as the wasting or degradation of space. And, since the growth of the big conurbations is faster than the growth of the urban population, a gap that will only increase in future, the negative effect on the ecosystem is destined to become further aggravated, unless there are robust corrective measures.

Humans' increased presence on the planet is a powerful contributor to modern climate changes, which are in turn the result of increased greenhouse gas emissions. This entails global warming, rising sea levels, the tropicalisation of the climate in temperate regions, and an increase in extreme climate events. This is a very intricate and technically complex

subject; here I will only touch upon it fleetingly. It has now
been proven that the increase in greenhouse gas emissions –
an increase due to growth in population and in human activities – is at the root of the global warming that has been under
way over the last several decades. As we read in the International Panel on Climate Change (IPCC)'s Fifth Assessment
Report: 'Anthropogenic greenhouse gas emissions have
increased since the pre-industrial era, driven largely by economic and population growth, and are now higher than
ever.'[8] This is not to say that human activity had no effects
on the climate in the preindustrial era; but it certainly had a
much more limited and localised impact. These climatic
effects may have been the consequence of extensive forest or
savannah fires, or perhaps – as in the case of the great metrop-
olis of London – of the thousands of chimneys pumping out
smoke from the firewood and coal burned by households and
workshops. In 1662 (just four years before the Great Fire of
London) John Graunt observed that London was 'not so
healthfull now as heretofore. It is doubted whether encrease
of People, or the burning of Sea-coal were the cause, or
both ... many People cannot at all endure the smoak of
London, not onely for its unpleasantness, but for the suffoca-
tions which it causes.'[9] This happened at a time when the
Industrial Revolution still lay far in the future.

Calculations tell us that between 1970 and 2010 there was
an 80 per cent increase in the volume of greenhouse gas emissions (four fifths of which are CO_2). All kinds of human
activity have contributed to this increase, from energy production to industry, agriculture, housing, trade, and transport. Some studies tell us that rising population numbers are
responsible for around a half of this increase. Naturally this
causal connection is mediated by the different economic conditions of various populations: the growth of a population
made up of people who emulate Simeon Stylites would have
practically no effects on greenhouse gas emissions, unlike a
high-income population made up of reckless consumers.
Indeed, we have concrete data to back up this argument:
between 1980 and 2005 the high-income countries contributed just 7 per cent to the world's population increase but 29
per cent to the rise in greenhouse gas emissions (CO_2), whereas
the low-income countries contributed 52 per cent to the

demographic increase and just 13 per cent to the rise in emissions.[10]

The IPCC makes complex global simulations based on hypotheses regarding population increase, economic growth, and the rise in emissions. The most recent such simulations have confirmed that the tendency towards global warming (almost one degree extra in 2000–10, by comparison to the mean for 1850–1900) will continue across the next century. Depending on different hypotheses of increases in emissions, by the end of the century (2081–2100) the globe's mean temperature will be between 1 and 4°C higher than it was in the 1986–2005 period.[11] Specialist publications explain the complex geophysical consequences of global warming, from the melting of the polar ice caps to rising sea levels, the desertification of vast regions, and changes in ocean currents. All of these things are of great significance for human society.

Before moving away from climatic questions – of interest in this chapter because population is an important factor in global warming – we might ask ourselves what impact the latter has had on the former. While a certain alarmism has arisen around this topic, it ought to be rather moderated, considering the human species' considerable ability to adapt to the climate. Indeed, we can find cases of humanity settling at the most varied latitudes and in the most extreme habitats ever since the Palaeolithic period, even without the protections that experience and technologies have gradually placed at humans' disposal over time. Today the almost 1 million inhabitants of Irkutsk live at an annual mean temperature of –1°C (and in January the average thermometer reading is –20°C). The inhabitants of Oman's capital Muscat, 29 degrees of latitude to the south of that Siberian city, live with a mean annual temperature that touches 30°C. This suggests that an increase of a few degrees, spread across almost a century, may not necessarily have major consequences. But such a conclusion is overly simplistic, obscuring many of the negative aspects that also need to be taken into account. First among these is the considerable variability of climate change across the different parts of the globe, which has a heavier impact on fragile or marginal areas. As we have seen, coastal areas in particular would be much more vulnerable to flooding, and this would have considerable negative consequences for their populations. Second comes the drying up of vast low-latitude regions and a loss of productivity in cereal cultivation. Third comes a geographic redistribution of pathogenic agents, along with an increase in certain infectious diseases and in malnutrition in the areas subject to the greatest warming. Lastly, forecasts speak of increased morbidity and mortality as a result of heatwaves, flooding, and droughts.

Anyone who has taken long-haul flights over deserted and unpopulated expanses of great countries and continents will know that the Earth is big and seemingly empty. Moreover, if everyone lived with a population density equivalent to that of the highly civilised Singapore, all humanity could concentrate in France and Spain, leaving the rest of the world deserted. If Italy be added, the three countries could also host the 3 or 4 billion people who will presumably be added to the current world population by the end of the century. But reality tells another story. Since the Industrial Revolution, population growth and the intensification of human activities have allowed us to see the finite character of the planet on which we live. Distances have shrunk – while Magellan and Elcano's expedition took three years to circumnavigate the world, today a supersonic plane does it in twenty-four hours – and the planet's physical limits are ever more evident. The fanning out of the human population exercises pressures on areas that are important for environmental balances, valuable for their landscape, or of a fragile nature. Slowing down demographic growth continues to be a priority, but the demography of the twenty-first century also poses a further problem to the international community: that of conserving the appropriate environmental balances and of restoring them where they have been compromised. These balances are threatened by a badly managed rise in the human activities of production and consumption. In a finite world, every extra person on this planet demands an extra share, however tiny, of the space that exists. This is the extra space necessary for food supply, housing, moving around, and enjoying the resources of the land and the environment. As the population rises, the use of space will need to respond more and more to criteria of rationality and fairness, respect for environmental balances, and waste reduction. The more the population grows, the more restrictive these limits will become, and the more important the responsibilities incumbent on individuals, communities, local and national governments, the international community. This is the ethical imperative that must guide us if we are to be able to hand a living, lively, and liveable planet down to future generations. Before the century is out, many more billions of people will have to find space on this planet.

3

Adaptation and Self-Regulation

- ◆ Demographic systems' adaptation and self-regulation
- ◆ Examples from history
- ◆ The possibility of regulating modern populations:
  Reproduction levels and migration
- ◆ Biological and social change
- ◆ Italy after the crisis: A system change?

'Most importantly, flee from the pestilential place, speedily, and return late and from afar.' Such was Marsilio Ficino's advice in his 1479 treatise *Contro la peste*. This is what the citizens of Florence and of many Italian and European cities had done during the century-long plague pandemic beginning in 1348, every time the hotbeds of disease flared up again and put lives at risk. Adopted by many, this behaviour also had consequences at a collective level. For it periodically emptied out the cities, and particularly their most affluent layers. Why talk of fleeing? Because in the face of difficult circumstances this was an elementary defensive strategy – and not the only one – guided by a survival instinct. A serious epidemic's negative consequences in terms of population loss could later be 'remedied' through increased nuptiality, a more intensive rate of marital births, and also a lower number of deaths. For the weakest and most fragile individuals had already been cut down by high mortality during the crisis.

The reactions mentioned above were contingent and immediate in nature. But the populations of the past – whose dynamic was constrained by natural factors (incurable diseases, the inability to control fertility) – had far from negligible capacities to adapt to changing circumstances. The concept of a 'demographic system' is useful for understanding how this might have happened. This term describes the ensemble of relations and interdependencies that link demographic phenomena together. For example, excessive reproduction could imply less parental care for each child and thus be linked to higher mortality; in consequence a large number of children would prove incompatible with high infant survival rates. Conversely, if reproduction were too low, this would sit badly with high mortality, because the effect would be to compromise a demographic group's family descent and vitality. Furthermore, it was possible for different demographic systems to arrive at an equal number of children per woman, if in the one system there was a low marriage age and a large proportion of women who did not marry, while in the other case all women did marry but at a higher age. Lastly, a system of demographic behaviours would remain stable so long as the intersection of factors determining each single variable did not change. That includes both internal factors, such as social and economic organisation, and external ones, such as space, available resources, climate, and disease. When these factors varied, the system could adjust and transform itself in order to adapt the demographic dynamic to the changed conditions. Many scholars, borrowing a concept from the natural sciences, maintain that populations have 'homoeostatic' self-regulation mechanisms that serve to stabilise their dynamics. However, this theory implies the existence of automatic mechanisms that are set in motion when the system is subjected to stress, through the operation of some hypothetical 'invisible hand'. But this theory is not a persuasive one, not least because history is full of examples where this sort of automatic mechanism did not come into operation. It seems better to consider self-regulation mechanisms as potential forces that can be set in motion in certain conditions but that can also fail.

History provides quite a few examples of demographic systems that change and adapt.[1] Some of these historical examples are a matter of conjecture, while others are grounded in solid factual evidence. There are some indications that the transition from hunting and gathering to agriculture brought about an acceleration in the previously slow demographic growth. Peoples living off agriculture benefited from the more regular availability of food and from stable settlements, which brought an increase in birth rates by comparison to those of hunter-gatherer populations.[2] Other examples are based on verified facts and are not a matter of conjecture. Europe's populations were cut by a third after the secular cycle of plagues that began in 1348, which brought profound structural changes: lower population density, greater availability of arable land, and the substitution of intensive cultivation by extensive cultivation and animal husbandry. Around the beginning of the sixteenth century the population levels recovered to what they had been two centuries previously, but the demographic structure was now different: it was characterised by a lower marriage age, the recomposition of households into larger units that contained more brothers' households, and perhaps also greater matrimonial fertility. In Japan, the long cycle of demographic growth during the first phase of the Tokugawa period in the second half of the seventeenth century and the early decades of the eighteenth was followed by a long stagnation, essentially based on the control of nuptiality and on infanticide. Another exemplary case is Ireland. Growing rapidly into a demographic system characterised by low marriage ages, the Irish population tripled between the beginning of the eighteenth century and the Great Famine of the 1840s. This massive crisis precipitated changes already visible in previous decades. A new demographic system now established itself, characterised by higher ages at marriage, a high level of celibacy, and a continual outflow of migrants. At the beginning of the twentieth century Ireland's population had fallen to slightly under a half of its levels before the crisis.

The knowledge of the past available to us does not always allow us to follow the mutations of a given demographic system. But it is equally telling to note the plurality of systems that prevail among different populations in a certain era.

Indeed, up until the twentieth century, a hypothetical line from Trieste to St Petersburg very clearly separated a Western European 'system' of low marital intensity from an Eastern European one with more extended families and high nuptiality. Also in Europe, areas affected by malaria – mainly in the Mediterranean and in the Balkans – were characterised by very high mortality and reproduction levels. This is what is defined as a 'high pressure' demographic system, sharply diverging from areas not affected by malaria. In America, demographic growth among communities of European origin had rhythms and modalities distinct from those of indigenous communities, and indeed from those of communities of African origin. China – which over time also underwent marked phases of growth and regression – saw the development of a demographic system in which couples had a range of choices with regard to matrimony, childbirth, and infanticide, which could be adjusted to the circumstances.

As I showed in Chapter 1, the long history of populations up to the modern Industrial Revolution was far from linear. The populations of the various regions and continents did slowly shift, but often not in synchrony, and this meant sometimes profound variations in the world's geodemography. As circumstances changed, the systems governing demographic change did not simply remain rigid, but rather took advantage of humans' great ability to adapt. However, on the whole, preindustrial populations had only modest capacities for growth, constrained by natural factors that governed survival and reproduction. The last two centuries have overturned the old balances, enormously strengthening the ability of individuals to make their own choices. One need only think of the way in which unions are formed. At one time they were subject to strict familial, religious, or civil rules. Today it is possible to conclude a union for reproductive purposes without (almost) any kind of constraints, and such a union can also be dissolved much more easily than it could in the past. As for reproduction, couples have ample discretion in deciding how many children they will have and when. Even if contraception fails, in a growing number of countries voluntary interruption of pregnancy is an accessible and legal practice. I might add that, while at one time legislation frequently raised barriers to people's ability to move around within a given country and to make their homes where they pleased, today this is considered to be the expression of a fundamental right. As I will go on to discuss, while this increased ability to move around does apply to migration within a given country, it does not similarly apply to international migration. It is worth making clear that this increase in individuals' capacity to choose certainly is a positive development. However, it is not necessarily guided by a benevolent 'invisible hand', and it can give rise to negative developments that themselves have to be corrected. One need only think of the serious negative consequences that very low birth rates create in numerous contexts. But this is a subject for discussion later on.

So far this ability to choose has not been achieved in the poorest countries, even if declining birth rates suggest that means of birth control are spreading and becoming more effective.[3] But this is not the case everywhere. Table 3.1 reports the number of children per woman in various regions and large countries around the world, in the mid-twentieth century and today.

Table 3.1 Mean number of children per woman in various regions and large countries

	1950–5	2010–15	Percentage change
Africa	6.6	4.7	−29
Egypt	6.6	3.4	−48
Ethiopia	7.0	4.6	−34
Nigeria	6.4	5.7	−11
Sub-Saharan Africa	6.5	5.1	−22
Asia	5.8	2.2	−62
China	6.1	1.6	−74
India	5.9	2.5	−58
Indonesia	5.5	2.5	−55
Pakistan	6.6	3.7	−44
Latin America and the Caribbean	5.9	2.2	−63
Brazil	6.2	1.8	−71
Mexico	6.7	2.3	−66

Source: United Nations, *World Fertility Report: Fertility at the Extremes*. New York, 2013

There is no evidence that birth control existed sixty years ago among any of the populations cited in table 3.1. Indeed, as a general rule we can deduce the presence of such controls wherever the mean number of children per woman is smaller than five.[4] In the present day, reproduction levels have fallen somewhere under two children per woman in China and Brazil. Across these two countries' respective continents as a whole – Asia and Latin America – the current level (2.2) is close to the replacement fertility rate, and consistent with a moderate rate of increase. The change in Africa as a whole, and particularly in the sub-Saharan region, has been relatively modest, as shown by an average of over five children per woman in this large and troubled region during the period 2010–15. Other studies add further interesting details on the major countries here under consideration. Table 3.2 relates the proportion of women of childbearing age (between 15 and 49 years) in these countries who use at least some form of pregnancy prevention, as well as the percentage of fertile and sexually active women in this same age bracket who are not using any means of contraception but do want to avoid or delay pregnancy ('unsatisfied demand for contraception'). They do not use contraception either out of ignorance about its methods or because

Table 3.2 Recourse to contraception in various regions and large countries

	Date of study	Contraceptive prevalence (%)	Unmet need (%)
Egypt	2006	60	12
Ethiopia	2010–11	29	26
Nigeria	2013	15	19
China	2006	85	2
India	2007–8	55	21
Indonesia	2012	63	11
Pakistan	2012–13	35	20
Brazil	2006	80	6
Mexico	2009	73	10

Source: United Nations, Population Division, *World Contraceptive Use*, 2014 (at http://www.un.org/en/development/desa/population/publications/ dataset/contraception/wcu2014.shtml)

the costs involved or family pressure prevents them from doing so.

Empirical studies demonstrate that, when at least three quarters of fertile and sexually active women use contraception, the average number of children will be close to the replacement fertility rate, or even below it. Such is the case in both China and Brazil. The smaller proportions using contraception in Pakistan or in African countries like Nigeria and Ethiopia show how slowly the changes are taking place in many poor countries. The percentages on 'unsatisfied' demand for contraception give an idea of the ground that social policy still has to make up. If 20 per cent of fertile and sexually active women in India do not want to have children but are not using contraception, that means that over 100 million women are prepared to change their behaviour. This could happen spontaneously and gradually, but the implementation of appropriate social practices could accelerate the process. I will return to this subject, but it is worth adding that these women – who want to limit the numbers of their offspring but do not know how, or are prevented from doing so – are feeding the recourse to abortion, which in most poor countries is legally allowed only in special cases (rape, duress, danger to the mother's life). According to a UN study,[5] in 2013 only 29 out of 144 developing countries allowed the interruption of pregnancy for either social or economic reasons or on demand. This holds for China, India, and Mexico, but none of the other nine major countries cited above.

Migration has always played a major role in demographic systems, as part of the processes adapting population growth to external constraints. The ability to move around is an essential element of human capital, and indeed one that humanity has employed throughout its history, ever since *Homo sapiens*'s diaspora outside of the African continent. We could even say that in the (very) long run the intensity of migration was inversely correlated to population density – at least so long as agriculture remained the main source of subsistence. As settlement has intensified and open spaces have diminished, the density of human population has risen and the opportunities for migration have been squeezed. Whatever limits migration faced in the past on account of logistical factors (difficulties in movement and transport, primitive communications networks), it did, however, make it possible to ease the pressure on resources in countries of origin, to populate new territories, to intensify settlements in less populated regions, and to develop new resources. The emergence and strengthening of nation-states, the stabilisation of an identity between the settled population and the citizens, and the hardening of geographic boundaries have placed certain constraints on long-range movements through the world's countries and regions. Yet this has not meant any abatement of the movements driven by the forces of expulsion and attraction at the root of migration.

The great transatlantic migration that spanned the nineteenth century and the first two decades of the twentieth is a classic example of an adaptation process in the demographic, social, and economic systems of the Old and New World. This was essentially an 'exchange' between a world rich in human capital and poor in resources (Europe) and a world rich in space and natural resources (America) that produced a migratory movement of tens of millions of people from the eastern to the western shore of the Atlantic. This migration can also be interpreted as a 'reaction', an 'adaptation' to accelerating demographic growth in Europe during the demographic transition process. Even once we have factored in emigration, the rate of increase in Europe's populations over the course of the nineteenth century reached 1 per cent per year. This was a rhythm many times faster than the average across the five previous centuries, and it was little compatible with the development potentials of populations that remained still largely rural.

In the seventy years since the end of the Second World War, migration processes have been heavily conditioned by political events: by the decolonisation process; by the division of the world into political blocs without mutual communications; by migration policies that in recent times have almost everywhere become more restrictive and selective; and by conflicts and their intersection with the flows of refugees. On the other hand the process of economic globalisation and the internationalisation of society have stimulated migration flows, even though these were restricted by national governments' policies. The 'choice' to migrate seems more difficult and problematic as an adaptive response to change than it was in the past. Nonetheless, in the last half-century the world's stock of migrants[6] has tripled (from 76 million in 1960 to 232 million in 2013), and it has increased also in relative terms. The increase has been most rapid in the developed countries, where absolute migrant numbers have quadrupled (from 32 to 136 million), thus marking a threefold increase as a share of the overall population.

There is also another way of evaluating how migration contributes to the equilibrium of demographic systems. Each society and each stable group of people has a population turnover that allows it to renew itself. Population turnover is both biological and social in nature. Biological turnover depends on forces of nature: birth and death. Social turnover, conversely, relies on the arrival and departure of foreigners – immigrants and emigrants. In the rich countries over the past half-century, population turnover has increasingly relied on this social factor, while the biological factor has proven inadequate. Let's consider the positive element of turnover: that is, new arrivals through birth and immigration. Across all the developed countries put together, 94 million babies were born in the five years between 1950 and 1955. Migration added almost nothing – around 1 million people, little more than 1 per cent of the total new arrivals.[7] Conversely, the five years from 2005 to 2010 saw the birth of just 70 million babies (in the meantime birth rates had fallen, even though the population rose by half), but immigration contributed some 17 million people, equivalent to 20 per cent of all new arrivals. In these six decades migration became a very significant – indeed, structural – element of the rich world's economic and social systems. And this took place despite the presence of growing barriers to movements between countries: so important are the factors that drive the movement of people – as the subsequent chapters will amply demonstrate.

A few pages back I referred to the reactions to crises in preindustrial eras. Their harmful effects above all rebounded on survival, and only indirectly on other demographic phenomena. Devastating old-style crises did take place even in the last century: leaving aside the ones linked to major conflicts, one need only think of the great famine in Ukraine and in Caucasian Russia in 1932–33 after forced industrialisation and collectivisation in the countryside; the equally bloody famine following the Great Leap Forward in China in 1959–61; and the one that struck North Korea in the second half of the 1990s.[8] The consequences of these crises and the reactions to them resemble those under the *ancien régime* in terms of the impact that spikes in mortality have on marriages, reproduction, family organisation, inward and outward migration, and demographic recovery in subsequent years. In the current era, in societies where behaviours are largely determined by individual choices, we see demographic systems responding and adapting to economic crises rather differently (under the *ancien régime*, when crises were not the result of epidemics, they were generally linked to crises in the rural economy). In general, the consequences that economic crises today have for survival and human health are relatively modest, while the effects related to marriages, family organisation, mobility, and migration are – or can be – significant. The great crisis that began in 2008 is still under way (even if there are some signs of normalisation). Once this crisis has been overcome and digested, it will be interesting to take stock of its consequences. These are of two orders: immediate ones and long-term ones, which can lead to significant changes in demographic systems. Already today (2015) the short-term 'responses' are partly visible.[9] Just to take the Italian case, we have seen a halt in the recovery of birth rates that had slowly been taking shape at the beginning of the century; a fall in marriages, but not in unions; an extension of the already exceptionally long amount of time children take to move out of the family home; reduced immigration; and increased numbers of people returning to their countries of origin (there is still a net intake of people, but it is notably lower than in the precrisis years). Conversely, there has been a rise in the numbers of native Italians who emigrate, most of them equipped with a good level of education (see Table 3.3).

We do not know what the responses to the crisis may be in the longer term and what possible lasting changes Italy's demographic system may undergo. However, we can make some conjectural predictions, which only the passing of time will allow us to verify. One hypothesis on migration holds that the drop-off in the demand for foreign labour may,

Table 3.3 The crisis's demographic effects on Italy: 2008 and 2016, compared

	2008	2016	Percentage change
Births (thousands)	577	486	–15.8
Deaths (thousands)	585	648	+10.8
Births per 100 deaths	98.6	75	–23.9
Marriages (thousands)	247	194	–21.1
Divorces	54	82	+51.9
Mean number of children per woman	1.45	1.34	–7.6
Life expectancy at birth (male/female)	81.3	82.4	+1.4
Total net immigration (thousands)	493	134	–72.8
Total net of Italian citizens alone (thousands)	–22	–65	+195.5

Source: Istat, National Institute for Statistics, Rome.
Note: The Italian edition covers changes between 2008 and 2014. Figures updated to 2016 and rate of divorces added for this edition.

as already in other countries, encourage further restrictions and the transition to a more selective migration policy, in the attempt to attract more skilled migrants or, as is commonly said, migrants with greater human capital. Moreover, the growth in the migration of Italians, especially to other European countries, could translate into a permanent outflow after the crisis – a sign of the younger generations' greater openness to working abroad, after a period of retreat into the national context lasting at least one generation. As regards the ordering and organisation of the family, one may suppose that the end of the crisis would bring a turnaround in young people's tendency to leave the family home later and later, reversing the trend we have witnessed during these last two decades of stagnation and recession. One may also suppose that the crisis in marriage rates – which has economic causes too, given the cost that the current 'form' of wedding ceremonies has reached – could make non-formal unions more frequent, given that they are both less expensive and less binding. Thus non-formal unions could become the normal form in which couples live together. Finally, as regards birth rates, one may conjecture that the end of the crisis may be followed by a return to a period when young people become autonomous sooner, which would bring forward their (currently exceptionally belated) decisions about their lives and reproductive choices. This could mean a recovery in couples' birth rates, as we had already begun to see in the twenty-first century before it was interrupted by the crisis.

In terms of population growth, it is well known that, given the current demographic parameters, in the absence of migration the total population of Italy will head into decline. In the long run this would have major negative consequences. The population would suffer an unsustainable decline, falling from today's 61 million to 45 million by 2050. Hence the dilemma: To what extent, and in what conditions, can an articulated and complex society like Italy's 'substitute' migrants for children? To what extent is Italy's very low reproduction rate the consequence of excessive investment in children (be it monetary, emotional, or psychological), an investment that seeks best 'quality' at the expense of 'quantity'? In the long run, the more limited the number of children, the greater will be the demand for migrants, accepted as a generic labour force that is not required to be of any great 'quality' in terms of studies, culture, or professional skills. I should add that these tendencies – the high level of investment in children and the migrants' low human capital – are heading in opposite directions, thus deepening the divide between migrant and autochthonous communities. In systems where individual choices guide behaviours, social policy faces a difficult task: unable to influence these behaviours directly, it can only offer incentives and disincentives or changes of context, in the hope that the desired effects will follow.

By way of a conclusion, let me set down some firm point of reference. It can be deduced from my discussion of the adaptation and regulation mechanisms that have guided or influenced the world's demographic developments. I introduced the concept of a 'system' – that is, the set of interdependencies between demographic phenomena that regulate how populations develop. I also made a distinction between an old, historical, or preindustrial regime, in which demographic systems were in large part determined by natural – biological and physical – factors, and a modern and contemporary system, in which demographic phenomena are heavily dependent on individual choices and freed from natural factors. Between the two systems – the old and the modern – stand the two centuries of demographic transition or demographic revolution during which individuals' ability to choose was empowered. This strengthened the demographic component of human capital. This transition is now complete in the rich world and in various less rich countries, but across large parts of the globe it still has a long way to go.

4

Sustainable ... for Whom?

- ♦ Zeus, the Brundtland Report, and sustainability
- ♦ The millennium development goals and the sustainable development goals: Isn't population a priority any more?
- ♦ Demographic explosion, demographic decline: Both unsustainable
- ♦ The parable of Tycoonia and Pauperia

There was a time when the countless tribes of men, though wide-dispersed, oppressed the surface of the deep-bosomed earth, and Zeus saw it and had pity and in his wise heart resolved to relieve the all-nurturing earth of men by causing the great struggle of the Ilian war, that the load of death might empty the world. (*The Cypria*, fragment 3 = scholion to Homer, *Iliad* 1.5; quoted from the volume *Hesiod, The Homeric Hymns and Homerica*, trans. and ed. Hugh G. Eve-lyn-White, London/New York: William Heinemann/G. P. Put-nam's Sons, 1920)[1]

This is how a post-Homeric poem introduced the theme of sustainability: the 'deep-bosomed earth,' 'all-nurturing' and yet oppressed by the 'countless tribes of men' – an always pressing theme. But the expansion of human activities, population growth, the cramping of the world, and the clear

perception of the world's limits have acutely put it back at
the centre of international debate. The question of sustainability is a powerful catalyst to some very old fears. According to the definition given by the 1987 Brundtland Report
(*Our Common Future*), sustainable development is development that 'meets the needs of the present without compromising the ability of future generations to meet their own needs'
(4.1).[2] The concept of sustainability was then further generalised, as it became tied up with the question of whether the
development of economic activities was compatible with safeguarding the environment:

> Environment and development are not separate challenges;
> they are inexorably linked. Development cannot subsist upon
> a deteriorating environmental resource base; the environment
> cannot be protected when growth leaves out of account the
> costs of environmental destruction. These problems cannot be
> treated separately by fragmented institutions and policies.
> (Brundtland Report, 2.40)

The principle of sustainability has been borrowed from the
natural sciences, where it refers to safeguarding the balance
and biodiversity of the environment. The extension of this
concept to economic development – and thus to the wider
social and political context feeding it – leaves its boundaries
indeterminate and makes it difficult to translate it into concrete actions. As a result, the concept of sustainability takes
on more of the character of an ethical principle or moral
warning than of a well-defined guideline to human action.[3]

These pages will discuss the question of sustainability with
reference to the population, its dynamics, and its component
parts. Population growth and its dimensions are closely
linked to a society's stability and renewal, the occupation of
space, the use of resources, food consumption, and the greenhouse effect – all of which are phenomena that threaten
sustainability and must be kept under control. This poses
crucial questions. Are today's demographic tendencies sustainable? And, if they are not, what concrete actions can we
propose?

From the Second World War onwards the demographic
question and the multiple relations between development and

the rapid growth of the world's population were at the centre of international debate. What was spreading here was a vivid concern for the environmental and social consequences of a historically unprecedented economic growth. With regard to its environmental consequences, there was a resurgence of neo-Malthusian hypotheses holding that non-renewable resources could become exhausted in a not too distant future. At the same time the consideration emerged that the strengthening of demographic qualities (or prerogatives) and the human capital connected with them were proceeding too slowly. The lack of control on birth rates produced generations in too large numbers, frustrating the attempts to improve their education; brought onto the labour market fresh waves of recruits doomed to unemployment; confined women to domestic activities; caused uncontrollable flows of migration towards the cities; and put resources under pressure. Added to this was the fact that the decolonisation processes had taken half the world's population out of the direct control of the historical great powers. This upset the existing geopolitical balances; moreover, it allowed these powers to relinquish their responsibility towards the populations they had once ruled over.

The debate was amplified by international institutions, at the centre of which stood the organisations dependent on the United Nations system. In general, these organisations sought to direct discussions, official declarations, and recommendations concerning social policies in a cautious manner. Dampers were placed on the objective of 'reducing' the rate of population increase (which between 1950 and 1990 had far exceeded 2 per cent a year in the poor countries). Indeed, in the best of cases this advocacy for reduced rates of population increase appeared to be an act of paternalistic preaching – rich countries speaking down to the poor ones. In the worst of cases it appeared as an arrogant imperialist attitude, prompted by fears that the third world could grow too much. Rather less controversial, however, were questions concerning the strengthening of demographic prerogatives. For example, how could individuals, couples, and families be convinced that controlling – putting brakes on – fertility was a suitable and advantageous choice for them? How could a connection be established between sex education, birth control, taking care of one's body, and appropriate nutrition? How could women's and infants' health be improved, tying together decisions on reproduction itself, the proper treatment of pregnancy, birth and the postpartum stage, and good practices for child-rearing and infant nutrition?

The UN-backed conferences on population in 1974 (Bucharest), 1984 (Mexico City), and 1994 (Cairo) confronted these questions as well as many others, approving by consensus final documents that contained declarations of principle, recommendations, and policy suggestions. The 1994 Cairo conference – the International Conference on Population and Development (ICPD) – concluded with the passing of a 'programme of action'.[4] This programme represented the international community's official position on the relations between population and development, what policies to undertake, and the financing of these policies by national and international donors and by governments.

Many of the conclusions of the Cairo Conference inspired the Millennium Declaration, a statement jointly made by heads of state and government in 2000. Moreover, several demographic goals were included among the eight 'millennium development goals' to be achieved by 2015.[5] There has been a mix of successes and failures in achieving the goals that were set in 2000.[6] An intense debate has followed over what new watchwords, goals, and objectives might guide government and international community action after 2015, together with a flowering of initiatives and documents that seek to reformulate development strategies, which, as the leitmotif of the current lexicon has it, must be sustainable in social, economic, and environmental terms. The criticism has been levelled that – apart from their other failings – the millennium development goals were not integrated into a coherent framework that respects the inseparable development–sustainability pair.[7]

Without wishing to enter an analysis of the possible strategies and watchwords for the post-2015 period (which I will discuss in Chapter 8) and their approval or formalisation by the international community, I will limit myself here to addressing just one aspect of this problem. It seems that population has slipped out of the circle of questions that need addressing – as if its future growth, distribution, and structure were of little relevance to the problem of sustainability. Yet by the end of the century between 3 and 4 billion extra people will be added on to the other 7 billion that live on the planet today. All this will involve greater population density, more land used up by construction and cultivation, a greater consumption of non-renewable energy and resources, more greenhouse gases in the atmosphere, and a higher pollution of rivers, lakes, and seas. While each of these phenomena results from a variety of causes, a particularly prominent factor is demography: the larger or smaller number of people who will need feeding, housing, heating, transport, and supply in the form of a growing volume of manufactured goods. In short, it would seem that the 1960s–70s' red alert on the possibility of the 'population bomb' going off has now been downgraded and that demographic matters are considered part of the normal vicissitudes that affect the planet and its load of humans. Does this mean that demography is no longer one of the primary sources of the world's problems?

This less alarmist vision of the relation between population and sustainability is in part the result of a more mature and balanced reflection on the subject, backed up by the slowing of the world's population growth. The rate of increase has almost halved by comparison to what it was in the 1970s (from 2 per cent in 1970–75 to 1.1 per cent in 2010–15), and this relative fall seems to be a well-established tendency, destined to continue. Even so, this quite reasonable revision does not justify other illusions that seem to be spreading and are worth our delving into.

The first illusion concerns the conviction that demographic 'behaviours' – reproduction, survival, mobility, migration – are destined to 'converge' around uniform models and that the macroscopic differences – between geographic areas and between ethnic, social, or religious groups – that were specific to the last century but still exist have a tendency to decline and disappear. Such a vision is based on several elements. In the first place, historical tendencies indicate that the differences between countries are indeed being attenuated through the maturation and then completion of the demographic transition. Secondly, it is believed that the progress of technology and of the biomedical sciences – together with the spreading of their fruits – should produce a convergence around a survival model characterised by high life expectancy. It is also believed that, in a system based on good longevity, reproduction itself should settle at around two children per woman, which in a large part of the world seems to be the desired level of offspring. Finally, globalisation processes and the withering away of the differences between countries in terms of demographic growth should first reduce and then cancel out the factors that drive migration.

It seems that these considerations guide the hypotheses underlying the United Nations' latest projections, authoritative forecasts that stretch up to 2100.[8] For example, they predict that by 2100 the net numbers of migrants from poor to rich countries will have fallen to a third of what they were at the beginning of the century, even as the world population almost doubles. The average number of children per woman, which currently ranges from barely one in some countries to around six in others, should recover in low-fertility countries and rapidly fall in high-fertility ones, the respective figures ranging from 1.8 to 2.2 by the end of the century. The 'scissors' of life expectancy at birth are currently wide open: they encompass approximately 85 years in the highest longevity countries and barely 40 in the countries with shortest life expectancy. However, this gap will also close significantly, with a reduced range of 70 to 95 years by 2100. Finally, by the end of the century the rate of world population increase will approach zero.

So then, can we envisage a world with a stationary population, composed of regions and countries that will also have stationary populations once the convergence around uniform behaviours is complete?

The second illusion is the child of the first. It imagines that, in a state of demographic standstill, the world's geodemography also ends up assuming a fixed structure. Yet this seems a highly unlikely prospect. The geographic distribution of the population has undergone major variations across history (as I mentioned in Chapter 1, and as I will discuss in more articulated fashion in Chapter 5). This was true even when birth rates and mortality were 'constrained' into ranges of variation limited by the lack of voluntary birth control, the very high rate of transmissible illnesses, and weak levels of migration. In the last centuries there have been yet stronger geodemographic changes, also because of the lack of synchrony between demographic transition processes in the various parts of the world. These changes will be even stronger in coming decades (and it will also be possible to venture some well-founded forecasts on the kind of changes these will be).

It is difficult to imagine a future in which demographic cycles are reduced to being a factor of little influence on the world's geodemography, as a result of the homogenisation of demographic behaviours around one prevalent model. This would have to be a model in which economic homogenisation reduces migration movements to almost nothing; a model in which the propensity to bring children into the world is free from the cultural and social particularities of countries and regions, even though these will surely remain strong; a model in which survival adjusts to a high-longevity pattern, free from the consequences of the volatility of diseases or of the changing economic constraints on health systems. We might also think that, even in a regime where the world's population is substantially stable, areas in phases of growth could coexist with areas in phases of decline. In that case the effect of population on planetwide imbalances (greenhouse gas, global warming, non-renewable resources) would indeed be cushioned – but not those problems, mainly social and economic, that single countries or regions would continue to face as they undergo sustained cycles of demographic growth or depression.

In our era, the populations of the rich world and a large part of those of the poor world enjoy high levels of survival and the demographic dynamic is guided above all by birth rates. The continuing decline of this dynamics at the planetary level is taken as a sign that over the course of the twenty-first century world population will tend to stabilise – although this is a hypothesis that I have already warned the reader against. In 1950 the average number of children per woman worldwide was around five, and currently it equals a half of that. But, because of the different temporal cadences of demographic transition – which came early in Europe, in the nineteenth century, and has just begun in sub-Saharan Africa – the differences between continents, regions, and countries have never been more profound than they are today. East Asia has

around 1.6 billion people with an average birth rate of less
than 1.6 children per woman – well below the replacement
fertility rate. Added to this is another half-billion of similarly
low birth rates in Central–Eastern and Southern Europe.
Taken together, these populations amount to almost 30 per
cent of the world's total. At the other extreme, around 1
billion people (practically all the inhabitants of sub-Saharan
Africa) have almost three times higher fertility rates, of
around five children per women. This means that a strongly
unsustainable dynamics would emerge if fertility rates are to
remain the same: consider, for example, that the population
of sub-Saharan Africa would triple by 2050. Also unsustainable would be the situation of Europe where the birth rate is
lowest: there, if nothing changes, the population would shrink
considerably. This would not be a problem, were it not for
the deepening diseconomies that would result from the rapid
aging of the population and the reversal of the age pyramid:
diseconomies inherent in a fragile productivity, vulnerable
pension and healthcare systems, and pressures on the balance
of public budgets. Analogous problems will come to a head
two or three decades later in East Asia, where the decline in
birth rates is a relatively recent phenomenon. Let me take
Germany – Europe's most populous country (not counting
Russia) – and Nigeria – Africa's most populous country – as
illustrative examples and compare their respective populations in 2015 with the figures predicted for 2050, on the
hypothesis that during these thirty-five years reproduction
rates in the two countries will remain constant and equal to
the current ones (see Table 4.1).

The unsustainability of self-perpetuating behaviours strikes
you in all its gravity.[9] In Germany the population of people
under 60 would fall by a third, while that of people over
80 would more than double; by 2050 these latter would be
greater in number than people under 20.[10] In Nigeria the
population would triple across all age ranges (those over
80 quadrupling in numbers). While in 2015 the Nigerian
population is more than double the German population, on
this scenario it would be eight times greater by 2050. By that
date the average age among Germans would be 54, against
17 among Nigerians. Any development model applied to
the two cases would produce depressing results: a structural

Table 4.1 Population in Germany and Nigeria, by age group (in millions), 2015 and 2050

	0–19	20–39	40–59	60–79	80+	total
			Germany			
2015	14.4	19.4	24.6	17.7	4.6	80.7
2050	10.7	14.5	17.4	18.5	10.8	71.9
Change %	−25.7	−25.3	−29.3	+4.5	+134.8	−10.9
			Nigeria			
2015	99.0	51.3	23.7	7.8	0.3	182.2
2050	277.5	139.3	67.2	24.0	1.3	509.3
Change %	+180.3	+171.5	+183.5	+207.7	+333.3	+179.5

Source: United Nations, *World Population Prospects*: The 2012 Revision, New York, 2013 (at http://esa.un.org/unpd/wpp/unpp/panel_population.htm)

weakening of Germany, with enormous welfare burdens and falling productivity, and generalised impoverishment in Nigeria, with a very heavy onus on environmental balances.

The post-2015 agenda should therefore address two lines of reflection and action. The first is the traditional one, contained and repeated in countless international declarations and documents. This is the path followed by the millennium development goals and concerns the actions to be pursued in order to encourage the control of reproductive processes. Thus it seeks to support the decline in birth rates, above all where they are very high.

The second line concerns a matter that has not been a priority so far – in fact quite the opposite: how it would be possible to avoid a further decline in birth rates in regions where they are already very low, how these processes can be prevented from spreading to other countries, and, finally, what actions should be taken in order to allow a recovery in birth rates. The asymmetry between these two lines of action resides not only in their opposite goals, but also the nature and replicability of past experiences. There are numerous examples of social and fiscal policies that promoted and sustained voluntary birth control. But there is very little experience of policies that succeeded in producing a lasting recovery in birth rates, and in any case the results of these policies were precarious and controversial. In sum, it is 'easy' to act so as to contain or reduce birth rates, but 'difficult' – if not impossible – to act so as to increase them.

The transition from high to moderate fertility is linked to factors that are known well enough, quite apart from the general improvement in a population's living standards. The key factors have been greater investment in children, with its beneficial effects on their health, survival, education, and formation; policies implemented in order to free women from their subaltern role; and the introduction of welfare measures that have freed the older generations from complete dependency on transfers from their own children. More specific and focused policies should reduce the proportion of women who do not have access to means of contraception (or are even unware of their existence). A recent document stated that these women should be provided 'a full range of safe, reliable and good-quality contraceptive services to meet these and other unmet needs, particularly among currently underserved and hard to reach populations, including adolescents and youth, free of discrimination and coercion'.[11]

In countries where birth rates are currently very low, there is a lukewarm consensus that we will see them gradually recover. Such is the position of numerous institutions and experts who author demographic projections and forecasts. It remains unclear why any such recovery should take place. Some argue that, since very low fertility generates harmful negative externalities, states can react by transferring resources to couples and families, thus inducing them to have more children. Even aside from the practicability of these policies – and experience shows that they would demand a very considerable amount of resources[12] – there is also a conflict that has to be resolved between the negative externalities that low fertility produces for society collectively and the economic benefits that having one child rather than two or two rather than three brings to the parents themselves. True, state transfers to families could rebalance the trade-off of costs and benefits, yet this would place a heavy burden on public finances and would be difficult to sustain in a historical period where public spending is coming under greater restrictions. In more developed countries, such factors as women's greater financial autonomy (more women in the labour market), a fairer gender division of domestic labour (more men working in the home or raising children), and policies, both intensive and extensive, designed to reconcile work with domestic and extradomestic responsibilities have a positive effect on birth rates. The right mix of measures supporting families, fiscal strategies, and normative measures can help bring birth rates back to levels both closer to the replacement fertility rate and more consistent with couples' ideals and expectations.[13]

Earlier on I mentioned the numerous documents that various high-level international working groups, agencies, and organisations have produced in order to set out a 'post-2015 agenda' on themes concerning development. While these papers have a variety of emphases, positions, and strategies, the term central to all of them is 'sustainable development' – the category supposed to inform all the actions taken at the local, national, regional, and planetary levels. In general they set themselves apart from similar documents in the past, even recent ones, which 'fell short by not integrating the economic, social, and environmental aspects of sustainable development as envisaged in the Millennium Declaration, and by not addressing the need to promote sustainable patterns of consumption and production'.[14] Another document starts out from the recognition that 'the scale of human impact on the physical Earth has reached dangerous levels more rapidly and disruptively than was foreseen by most in 2000'[15] However, these and other documents do not explicitly state what effect demographic growth – the 3 or 4 billion extra people to be added to the world population by 2100 – will have on sustainable development. And yet, if demographic growth does indeed continue at the expected rate, then sustainability will be under serious threat.

Let me dwell a little on this point with the help of a fictitious example: two imaginary countries and their development up till 2050. Let me call them Pauperia and Tycoonia. Pauperia has a high rate of demographic growth, equivalent to a 2 per cent average increase between 2015 and 2050 (the same increase that the UN forecasts for Africa over this very period). In Tycoonia, by contrast, the population will remain stationary. Pauperia's GDP per capita is predicted to increase rapidly, by around 5 per cent a year, and experts argue that it can sustain this rate over the next thirty-five years. But, since the physical impact on the land is a function of the combination between the population and its degree of economic affluence (its income, or product), a simple multiplication tells us that over the next thirty-five years this impact will double in Tycoonia (all other things being equal) but will multiply twelve times in Pauperia. We know that technological development tends to 'decouple' economic growth from unsustainable means of production and consumption: that is to say, with more technology, each extra unit of production or consumption will take up less non-renewable energy and resources.[16] It is possible that this will indeed happen in Tycoonia, with the potential dematerialisation of consumption (an extra euro's spending might buy an e-book, access to a museum, or a haircut). But it is rather less likely to happen in Pauperia, where each extra euro will be spent on fuel for heating, cooking, and transport, on food for eating, on tools for working, on shoes for walking, and on other basic goods that cannot – or can only very slightly – be dematerialised.

If one wants to take this discussion to a deeper level, it would be worth deploying a synthetic index that can be obtained by calculating the amount, in tonnes per year, of basic resources 'extracted' and thus presumably consumed per head of population (i.e. including biomass, minerals, inert construction waste, energy materials).[17] This is called the 'metabolic rate'. Well, in the year 2000, the consumption equivalent to 20 tonnes per capita in the developed countries would have been more than triple that of the poor countries. These data confirm something that we already knew well: that rich countries' contribution to depleting the reserves of non-renewable resources is proportionally greater than their share of overall population. As for the future, it is worth noting that in the rich countries substitution processes, recycling, and the adaptation of consumption models will bring a reduction in the amount of energy and raw materials that corresponds to each extra euro's worth of production. What is more, over the next decades the populations of these countries are going to grow slowly or remain stationary. Therefore there is some basis for forecasting a stabilisation, or even a decline in the consumption of basic resources. But there are rather different prospects for the poor countries, whose incomes are a small fraction of incomes in their rich counterparts. In the decades to come their rate of development should exceed that of the rich economies, since the gap between the well-being of these two worlds should become relatively (if not absolutely) narrower, so long as the speed of population growth does not eat up the required investment. It is hoped that over the next generation the GDP per capita of these economies may increase two or three times over; and this will mean more iron for utensils, more fabric for clothing, more timber for construction, more space to live in, and more energy for this whole range of activities. Since poor populations' living standards are very low, this additional provision of personal goods will be the result of high inputs of energy, raw materials, and space per euro of extra product. Naturally enough, these populations aspire to more food, utensils, clothing, habitations, and fuel. Given that within two generations they will be 3 billion more numerous and that the provision of goods for each person will be many times greater, it is easy to understand that this growth – necessary though it is – cannot be sustained in the long run.

The logic of the so-called 'environmental Kuznets curve' (which is inspired by some of the ideas that the economist Simon Kuznets voiced in the 1950s) can help us in interpreting the tendencies currently at work. The curve predicts that, as incomes rise, the (material, energetic) content of each unit of production will grow, but at decreasing rates, until it will ultimately reach a turning point beyond which each further income unit will take up a decreasing amount of resources. The curve thus takes the shape of a bell or, better, of an upturned bowl. In the long run even the poor countries – which will no longer be poor – will be able to follow the downward part of the curve, just as is already beginning to happen (at least for some forms of consumption) in the rich countries. But it takes several generations and the onset of stagnation in population numbers for this process to put a halt to the growth in the consumption of basic resources. Table 4.2 reports the data of a United Nations Environment Programme (UNEP) simulation of metabolic rates in rich and poor countries, further subdivided into countries of higher and lower population densities (and there are structural

Table 4.2 Metabolism (extraction of basic resources) in the rich world and in the poor world, from 2000 to 2050

	2000	2050 hypothesis A	2050 hypothesis B
Population (billions)	6.0	8.9	8.9
Total metabolism	49.0	141.0	70
Metabolic rate			
Worldwide	8	16	8
Rich, high density	13	13	6.5
Rich, low density	24	24	12
Poor, high density	5	13	6.5
Poor, low density	9	24	12

Source: United Nations Environment Programme (UNEP), *Decoupling Natural Resource Use and Environmental Impacts from Economic Growth: A Report of the Working Group on Decoupling to the International Resource Panel*, 2011 (at http://www.gci.org.uk/Documents/Decoupling_Report_English.pdf)
Note: Total metabolism = billions of tonnes of materials extracted per year. Metabolic rate = tonnes extracted per person per year.

reasons for the latter to have higher rates of consumption). Figures are given for the years 2000 and 2050, and according to two different hypotheses. On the first hypothesis, nothing changes except for the rise in population numbers (metabolic rates remaining constant); the second hypothesis (moderate convergence and contraction) foresees a halving of metabolic rates in the rich countries, by way of innovation processes (as happens in the downward phase of the Kuznets curve) and a moderate increase of around one third in the metabolic rates in poor countries (in the upward phase of this same curve).

If nothing changed (hypothesis A: metabolic rates remained constant), the resources extracted would triple (or almost triple) over the half-century in question. If, on the contrary, there were a convergence between rich and poor countries and a contraction in the material content of each production unit (hypothesis B), then the extraction of resources would increase by 'only' 43 per cent.

This example shows how, in poor countries, the combination of economic and population growth will have a very serious, if not unsustainable impact on the environment in coming decades, as shown in the parable of Tycoonia and Pauperia. This creates two obvious general priorities. The first one is to accelerate investments in technology and the transfers of technologies from more developed countries to poorer ones (especially those that do not heavily displace the workforce). The second priority is to slow down the pace of demographic growth. I have already noted that, if birth rates in sub-Saharan Africa remain constant, by 2050 its population will triple (rising from 0.96 to 2.75 billion), whereas, if they fell from the current 4.8 children per woman to 2.6 by 2050 (at the bottom end of UN forecasts), its population would 'only' double (reaching 1.92 billion). To put it bluntly, by 2050 a variation of one child per woman will be 'worth' a variation in population numbers of approximately 380 million.

This is good reason to boost and strengthen those social policies that will encourage the transition towards more moderate levels in reproduction rates.

As I argued from the outset, for any discourse concerning sustainability, pushing down birth rates must remain a central priority. On the other hand, improving human capital (of which, to repeat, demographic prerogatives are an integral part) also prepares the ground for a response to the other priority, namely technological development. So now, let's make it clear: the demographic question must remain central to the debate on sustainability.

5

Geodemography and Geopolitics

- ◆ Mussolini: Numbers mean power
- ◆ The pendulum of fear, between growth and decline
- ◆ Geodemography and geopolitics
- ◆ The weight of numbers within states: Ethnicities, religions, minorities, and majorities
- ◆ Power rankings

'Some fool says "there's too many of us". The intelligent reply: "there's not enough of us". I say that Nations' demographic power is not merely fundamental to their political power, and thus their economic and moral power, but its very precondition.' Thus spoke Mussolini in his Ascension Day speech in May 1927.[1] In the 1920s and 1930s the human losses from the First World War, the declining birth rates in the richest countries, and the prospect – however distant – of demographic decline appeared to be indices or proofs that western civilisation was reaching its twilight. The question of the relationship between the power of nations and their population numbers – posed so directly and brutally by Mussolini – has long been the object of debate, assuming multiple different forms over time. The dominant way of thinking has swung like a pendulum between positive and negative visions of numbers and growth. In the seventeenth and eighteenth centuries mercantilism had upheld the view that having a numerous and growing population was both favourable and necessary, an advantageous factor from a political, economic, and military angle. A nation's wealth was linked to its numbers and to the margin that existed between the consumption of its mainly rural population and the value of what was produced. Through the imposition of taxation, this margin would increase the state's resources, and thus its power. However, already in the eighteenth century the mercantilists' convictions were beginning to fall apart, and the idea that population growth was determined by the avail ability of subsistence resources – and was not a positive factor just by itself – again gained ground. This was the context in which Thomas Malthus produced his writings, decisively swinging the pendulum towards the more negative interpretation: the lack of preventive checks on population growth placed pressure on resources and activated the negative checks capable of bringing the population down to lower levels. Across much of the nineteenth century, Malthus' position, in deepened and articulated versions, permeated writings on economics and society. If the world is finite and land is finite, then demographic growth cannot continue without limit. Malthus' interpretation inspired Darwin and contributed to the theory of evolution and natural selection, considered as a consequence of the struggle for survival. The idea gained ground that in a finite world with open spaces humans, just like animal species, need living space – *Lebensraum* – which they can occupy and settle in. Elaborated by the zoologist, geographer, and anthropologist Friedrich Ratzel,[2] this concept was later adopted and distorted by Nazism and other dictatorial regimes. During much of the nineteenth century, still punctuated by subsistence crises, shortages, mass emigration, and the emergence of new forms of poverty, the growth of population and of its numbers continued to take on far from positive connotations.

But the pendulum was about to swing the other way. As the illustrious social scientist Jacques Bertillon wrote in 1897: 'In fourteen years Germany will have twice as many conscripts as France; then that people which detests us will devour us.'[3] The wounds of France's military defeat to the Germans at Sedan in 1870 had still not healed. Birth rates, which had already been falling in France since the beginning of the nineteenth century, now started to decline in the most developed parts of Europe. Demography became politically significant: Europe had exported millions of migrants to the other continents and the 'Great Powers' had built extensive colonial empires, belatedly to be imitated by Germany, Italy, and Japan. Numbers and space became important elements of geopolitics. There was a pervasive attention to, and even preoccupation with, the increasingly widespread fall in birth rates. Policies to drive up birth rates were implemented in various countries, and not only in those governed by dictatorships. The claim that Germany needed 'living space' became the pretext for Nazi expansion in Europe. A link was established between population numbers and military power, international influence, and territorial expansion. Mussolini's Ascension Day speech was a good barometer of a very widespread sentiment.

The pendulum would swing both back and forth once again after the Second World War. There was a strong recovery of demographic growth, fuelled by the baby boom of the 1940s–1960s; the definitive statistical discovery of a poor world with a high rate of increase; the decolonisation that liberated a large part of that world from the direct political control of the West; sensitivity to the dangers of environmental degradation; and concern over the possibility of non-renewable resources getting exhausted. Population numbers and growth took on negative connotations. Tellingly, the 1970s concluded with the birth of China's one-child policy, which aimed to slow and eventually overturn demographic growth. This meant that the world's most populous country was openly recognising that large numbers and rapid growth are a primary factor of weakness, not of strength.

The last swing of the pendulum came in the past two or three decades. As at the beginning of the twentieth century, the fear of demographic decline is reappearing today. It is fed by the decline in birth rates, which have sunk well below the replacement fertility rate in a good part of the developed world, and by the spread of analogous reproductive behaviours in many countries of the poor world, as well as by the recognition that low reproduction rates are not easily shifted by social and economic policies that seek to revive them, compromising both development and people's well-being.

These references to developments in thinking and opinion (most of them born and elaborated in the West) with regard to the value and meaning of population numbers and demographic change, swinging as they did between an optimistic and a pessimistic pole, provide a framework for the introduction of some empirical data. While the claim that 'numbers mean power' may be rather crude, it does contain elements of undeniable if banal truth. Already in the previous chapters I extensively discussed the varying speeds with which demographic change has manifested itself in the world's different continents and subcontinents. Figure 5.1 gives a general idea of the variations in the weight of different territories'

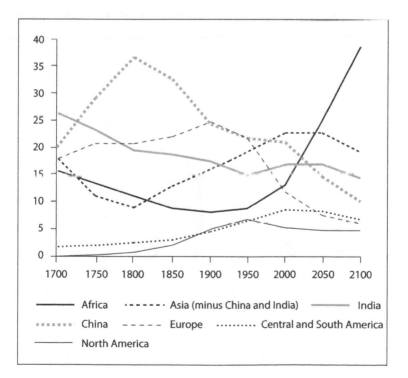

Figure 5.1 The continents', China's, and India's share of world population (%), 1700–2100

populations (as a percentage of world population) over the last three centuries and over the rest of the twenty-first century. Bear in mind that, as we look back in time around 1700, our quantitative estimates become more uncertain, just as they become increasingly uncertain towards 2100, as we forecast change in future decades. The lines in the graph are the expression of huge upheavals: what particularly sticks out is the declining weight of China, which reached its zenith at the beginning of the nineteenth century, and of Europe, which peaked in the early twentieth century. What also sticks out is – as we know – the great jump in the weight of the African population, beginning in the mid-twentieth century and possibly continuing at a sustained rhythm across the rest of this century.

In Figure 5.2 the timeframe is restricted to the century between 1950 and 2050, two thirds of which have already come and gone. Taken into consideration are three dates

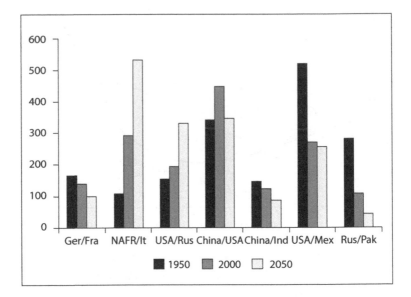

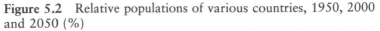

Figure 5.2 Relative populations of various countries, 1950, 2000 and 2050 (%)
Ger = Germany; Fra = France; NAFR = North Africa; Rus = Russia; Ind = India; Mex = Mexico; Pak = Pakistan

(1950, 2000 and 2050) and the relative population sizes of
various different countries, some of which are geographically
close, and in any case in some form of competition or potential conflict. In three cases (USA and Mexico, North Africa
and Italy, Russia and Pakistan) these are populations divided
by the fault line that separates the rich world from the poor
world, and the world with an early demographic transition
from the world with a belated one. The graphs show an
extraordinary degree of change. While in 1950 Italy and
North Africa had almost equal populations, by 2050 the
latter will be five times bigger; while the United States was
five times more populous than Mexico in 1950, by 2050 this
advantage will have reduced to just 2.5 times (though across
the twenty-first century each will increase at more or less the
same speed); and, while Russia was three times as populous
as Pakistan in 1950, by 2050 it will be three times smaller.

Also of interest are the relative populations of the big
global competitors. The United States' population was one
and a half times bigger than Russia's in 1950 (assuming
present borders; however, the USSR was 20 per cent more
populous at that point) but by 2050 it will be over three times
larger. China's size relative to the United States is the same
at the end of this period as at the beginning (with the Chinese
population over three times larger than the American one),
but only after having peaked at the turn of the millennium
(when it was around four and a half times larger). Equivalent
to one-fifth of the Chinese population in 1950, a century later
the Russian population will only be one-tenth as big. China's
population was 45 per cent bigger than India's in 1950, but
by 2050 will be 21 per cent smaller. Finally, not far beyond
the middle of this century France will turn the demographic
tables on its once bitter enemy – and today's peaceful partner
– Germany. By that point France will have regained its demographic lead over its neighbour, lost at the end of the nineteenth century. Jacques Bertillon will have his revenge.

Are the data summarised in Figures 5.1 and 5.2 simply a
statistical 'diversion'? What weight do demographic factors
have in determining a country's power, influence, or predominance over neighbouring or competitor countries? How
about in terms of defining the geopolitical landscape? Many
would say that these factors are only of marginal importance.

Small countries and small nations have played front-rank roles on the international stage; David-like, they have militarily defeated Goliaths, they have become powerful economic and financial leaders, and they have even colonised continents. Athens, Venice, the Netherlands, England, Portugal, Qatar. For the sake of avoiding insubstantial arguments and debates, we might sign up to the view offered by an illustrious demographer in the influential *Foreign Affairs* magazine at the end of the Second World War:

> Let us agree that position, resources, technical skills, economic and political organization, the psychological characteristics of the people, national aims, leadership and doubtless many other factors in addition to the size of population are components of political power and national influence. Let us agree also that numbers do not always count in the same direction – that Alaska would be stronger with more people but that India and Java might be stronger with half their present populations. It remains true that at relatively equal levels of economic development sheer numbers count heavily in political strength.[4]

There is also an intense debate on the influence that population numbers and demographic growth have within countries and nations. Although this 'geopolitics' can also influence international events, it is national more than international in scope, and is often linked to ethnic and religious divisions and to the arbitrary nature of the borders set down in the colonial era. Palestine is the best known and most resounding case in point. Notwithstanding the strong expansion of the Jewish population on account of high birth rates (that is, relatively higher than the West's) and continuing immigration, the Arab Palestinian population is growing far faster. If we look at the whole territory of what was once Palestine under the British Mandate, we see that the Arab component (the population of the current territories of Gaza and the West Bank, plus well over one-fifth of the population of the State of Israel) will surpass the Jewish population around 2020, and will then continue to increase this advantage. Any peaceful solution of this matter – whatever the contours of the agreement that is ultimately reached, and whether it prescribes a one-, two-, or three-state solution or the transfer of populations or territories – will have to have the demographic question at its very centre. In Lebanon the presence of both Christians and Muslims led to a constitutional order balanced across the different communities, notwithstanding the variation in their respective weight among the general population. While in the mid-twentieth century this balance favoured Christians, today it has sharply rebounded in favour of Muslims. The differential demographic growth of Syria's various ethno-religious groups adds yet further complications to that country's tragedy, and the higher birth rates and population growth among the Kurds is a cause for persistent underlying concerns in Turkey. In Europe there are growing fears over the immigration of Islamic populations, which are perceived as a rising tide that threatens the continent's cultural identity and social peace. This fear translates into dangerous racist tendencies. The data show that Muslim communities are indeed rising in numbers: in the EU-27 they amounted to 10.4 million people in 1990 and to 19.1 million in 2010 (an 83 per cent rise) on account of increased immigration (especially in Spain and Italy) and of higher birth rates among Muslim couples.[5] We might reasonably expect the rate of increase to lessen over the two decades from 2010 to 2030, also because immigrant communities' reproductive preferences will converge with those prevalent among native populations. We can assume that Europe's Muslims will not be more than 30 million in number by 2030. Certainly they will represent a significant minority (5–6 per cent of the population), but it is a far cry from there to fearing that the tide would submerge European civilisation.

History is rich in cases of ethnic or religious conflicts fuelled by the changing demographic relations within a given country: examples range from the *revanche des berceaux* ('revenge of the cradles') in French-speaking Quebec – whose high birth rates contributed to the challenge to English-speaking predominance in Canada – to the conflict between Catholics and Protestants in Northern Ireland. Even the US constitution was concerned to balance the relative electoral influence of the northern states and the more populous southern ones by giving lesser weight to blacks, who were more numerous in the South.[6] Today there is a lively debate on the social, cultural, and political–electoral consequences of the rapid growth of America's 'minorities'. According to the Census Bureau, already in 2011 there were more births to Hispanic, African American, and Asian parents than to whites ('Caucasians'); this same institution estimates that in 2044 'minorities' will become the 'majority' of the entire population. This is a historical change for a nation born from the womb of European society and deriving its language, culture, and institutions from British models. Its effects could well transcend national borders, strengthening (for example) the United States' relations with Spanish- and Portuguese-speaking Latin America. These are just a few of the countless examples provided by both ancient and modern history regarding the political consequences of differential demographic growth. But they are most of all matters internal to particular countries, of only limited importance to the international picture that interests me here.

Scholars of geopolitics have rightly recognised the effects of changes in populations' age structure and the political consequences following from them. For example, it has been argued that the large number of young people unable to tolerate corrupt and authoritarian regimes was a powerful factor in the upheavals in the Mediterranean region that fanned out from the so-called 'Arab Spring'. While the lack of similar outcomes in other parts of the poor world with analogous demographic characteristics is worth noting, it is true that the number of young people (I mean here those between 15 and 35 years of age) in Tunisia, Libya, Egypt, and Syria tripled between 1970 and 2010, rising from 30 per cent to a 35–40 per cent share of the overall population over this same period. Perhaps the most important consideration is that these young people are not only more numerous than they were in the past, but also highly educated; they live mostly in urban areas and are affected by the gap between expectations and reality more than previous generations were.

It may sound dangerous to speak of 'national power'. This nineteenth-century expression is evocative of clashes between the great powers for the sake of dividing up land and resources, carving up spheres of influence, and dominating the weaker countries. It sounds dated – like a sort of positivism applied to international relations – to attempt to measure 'power' by using objective parameters and then deduce from that which countries are more or less powerful. Since the end of the Second World War, we have concerned ourselves rather with measures of individual or collective degrees of social or economic well-being. Yet there is very widespread interest in the objective measurement of 'national power'; there is a developed 'power metric'; and there are serious, well-financed bodies and think tanks with public funding (in North America, Europe, China, and India), which make use of complex algorithms to compile international rankings and to provide estimates aimed at defining potential scenarios and strategies. Two indicators always included in such measurements of power' are, for obvious reasons, the number of inhabitants and the GDP. The United States and China are always at the top of the various rankings. Table 5.1 shows the top ten countries (as well as Italy's place) in rankings based on [each of] these variables. The classification of the top ten countries by population is very different in 2015 and in 2050: Nigeria will rise from seventh to fourth place, while the Democratic Republic of Congo and Ethiopia will enter the top ten, in place of Russia and Japan. Production is considered either in terms of GDP, calculated at market prices and translated into US dollars at current exchange rates, or else GDP as based on purchasing power parity (PPP). This way of measuring GDP is a convention that takes into account the fact that the prices for identical goods or services are different in different countries, and are usually higher in rich countries than in poor ones. A haircut or a bowl of soup may cost 1 dollar in a poor country and 20 dollars in a rich one, but they have the same utility for the consumer. Not to take account of this is to underestimate poor countries' 'well-being' and to overestimate that of rich countries.

The two GDP rankings (the second and third columns) feature considerable differences. While in terms of nominal GDP India ranks tenth, it rises to third place in terms of GDP (PPP); France, on the contrary, falls from fifth to ninth place; Mexico rises to the top ten; and so on. In 2014 the news, from the International Comparison Program (ICP), that China had overtaken the United States in terms of GDP (PPP) created great stir in the newspapers. This would mean that, in 2014, 317 million Americans had a total domestic purchasing power equivalent to that of 1.356 billion people in China

Table 5.1 Ranking of countries by population, production, development assistance, and other indicators of 'power'

Ranking	Population	Nominal GDP	PPP GDP (Purchasing Power Parity)	ODA (Official Development Assistance)	CINC (Composite Index National Capability)	NPI (National Power Index)	GFP (Global Fire-power Index)	NSI (National Security Index)	CNP (Comprehensive National Power)
	2013	2013	2013	2012	2012	2010	2014	2007	2005
1	China	USA	USA	USA	China	USA	USA	USA	USA
2	India	China	China	UK	USA	China	Russia	China	UK
3	USA	Japan	India	Germany	India	France	China	Norway	Russia
4	Indonesia	Germany	Japan	Japan	Japan	UK	India	Russia	France
5	Brazil	France	Germany	France	Russia	Germany	UK	India	Germany
6	Pakistan	UK	Russia	Sweden	Brazil	Russia	France	Japan	China
7	Nigeria	Brazil	Brazil	Norway	Germany	Japan	Germany	S. Korea	Japan
8	Bangladesh	Russia	UK	Holland	South Korea	Italy	Turkey	UK	Canada
9	Russia	Italy	France	Canada	UK	Canada	S. Korea	Germany	S. Korea
10	Japan	India	Mexico	Australia	France	Spain	Japan	France	India
(Italy)	23	9	11	11	11	8	12	28	n.d.

Sources (by columns): United Nations; International Monetary Fund; OECD; http://www.correlatesofwar.org/COW2%20Data/Capabilities/nmc3-02. htm; http://nationranking.wordpress.com/category/national-power-index; http://www.globalfirepower.com; Karl Kwang, *Measuring Geopolitical Power in India: A Review of the National Security Index* (NSI), CIGA WP 136/2010; http://en.wikipedia.org/wiki/Comprehensive_National_Power

(that is, a population four times the size). But this news had little relevance (or none at all) where the two countries' international weight was at stake; China's GDP, calculated at market prices, is still only three fifths of the US GDP. Indeed, what matters in international relations is not so much the GDP-PPP as the GDP calculated at market exchange rates, though it is well known that this presents many other disadvantages, since exchange rates can be manipulated or can vary significantly. It is US dollars – or euros, yen, or pounds sterling – that allow the purchase of raw materials and strategic foodstuffs (oil, copper, rice, grain) or similarly vital manufactured goods (computers, planes, machinery, software). In conditions of equal development, a large country can devote a lot more resources to cooperation and development assistance than a small country can, by diverting funds to support education and research, by creating infrastructure, and by purchasing food or medicine – in short, resources capable of creating well-being, health, and knowledge. However, the opposite is also true, and these resources can have destructive effects. They may be devoted to armament in the form of buying fighter planes, missiles, or artillery (in the five years between 2009 and 2013 more than a half of worldwide arms exports were concentrated in the United States and Russia alone). For better or for worse, a country with a large population count for much more on the international stage than a small country does.[7] The amount of resources for official development assistance (ODA) is another telling indicator of a country's influence abroad. The ODA rankings (Table 5.1), however, refer only to OECD countries, thus excluding China, India, Saudi Arabia, Qatar, Venezuela, and other states that transfer large amounts of resources to other countries in different ways. Small countries such as Norway, Sweden, and Holland transfer greater amounts of funds than much larger countries such as Australia, Canada, and Italy. In this way they acquire greater importance in the field of international relations, uncoupling the question of their influence from the demographic and economic dimensions alone. There are also many composite indicators of the 'power of states', which have been developed by various research centres scattered across the globe. The last four columns in Table 5.1 show the rankings of the ten most influential countries according to five indicators designed by a variety of study groups – indicators that synthesise states' military, defence, and security capabilities.[8]

Comparing the various rankings would be a tedious task, of little merit. They employ different methodologies, are designed for distinct purposes, and do not refer to the same year. Certainly it is no surprise that the United States and China are at the head of the rankings and India in a strong position: ultimately population numbers and the size of the economy dominate over other variables. However, the role played by population remains ambiguous. Over time, in a world where the inequalities between countries are narrowing, population numbers would play a decisive role in shaping the geopolitical order. Yet over the last half-century of globalisation these inequalities appear to have become stronger. Uncontrolled demographic expansion has its own costs, which can translate into economic and social fragility. In previous centuries the sheer numbers of a country's peasant workforce could well increase the state's economic power – as the mercantilists argued – or fuel its military power (France in the era of the Napoleonic Wars was the most populous country in Europe, not counting Russia). The various technological revolutions – steam, electricity, the internal combustion engine, electronics, IT – have undermined the primary importance of population numbers. The quality of human capital, its capacity to innovate, produce culture and technology, and spread them around the world is undoubtedly pre-eminent. One very recent study[9] ventured a forecast of the different levels of education achieved by the various age groups of the world's population. Today the rich world's numerical disadvantage is (at least in part) compensated by the higher level of education – and hence of human capital. However, this divide will largely have been bridged within the space of a generation. In the next decade India's number of inhabitants will surpass China's, and over the following thirty years it will also catch up with China's education levels, which are considerably higher today. Moreover, at equal degrees of development, a populous country will be better able than other, less populous ones to mobilise critical masses of capital for strategic investment; to bring together considerable numbers of researchers able to bring about innovation;

to build networks of cultural production centres that should spread culture elsewhere in the world; and to guide lifestyles and influence other societies beyond its own borders.

Our current century's powerful demographic dynamism will not be without effect on the global geopolitical order. This will be true especially if the gifts of technology and human capital, which are today the privilege of the rich world, move towards the poor world. While the United States' vibrant demography will shore up its primacy in the world, the opposite will happen with Europe and Russia. The Indian subcontinent's position will be strengthened, China's weakened. The sub-Saharan continent will become increasingly central, if not pre-eminent, as long as its demographic growth does not bear the seeds of destruction – in case it proves difficult or impossible to devote resources to investment by taking them away from a rapidly growing population.

6

Homo sapiens, Homo movens

- Shipwrecks and barriers
- International migration grows despite obstacles
- Demographic and economic pressures
- Three globalisation processes in the past, and the fourth one to come
- The unsustainability of politics without international rules

A hundred years ago general Felipe Angeles, a heroic protagonist of the Mexican Revolution, joked with his comrades as they stood at the border at Nogales: "'I'm going to the United States", he said as he stepped forward, and then as he stepped back again "I'm coming back to Mexico".'[1] This was a porous border, or rather a non-border. Today a solid barrier several metres high runs along a third of the 2,000-mile border that separates Mexico from the United States, leaving animals and – most importantly – people unable to cross it.[2] Similar barriers separate Israel from the State of Palestine, Turkey from Greece, the Spanish enclaves of Ceuta and Melilla from Morocco, and South Africa from Mozambique, to give just a few examples. Others are planned in hotspots around the world.

In 2016 over 5,000 migrants died in Mediterranean waters as they desperately attempted to save their lives and escape war and persecution by reaching European shores. This Mare Nostrum [Mediterranean] Passage today is almost as risky and bloody as was the Middle Passage between Africa and the New World for the slaves on the transport ships of the seventeenth and eighteenth centuries. One international organisation calculates that, since the year 2000, some 40,000 migrants have died attempting to reach another country and that, for every recorded death, there are two more that remain uncounted.[3]

Militarised borders and dead migrants are the two most obvious pathologies of a global migration system that is left to the whims of forces as pervasive and powerful as they are difficult to govern. Yet migration is one of the vital forces that have driven the world ever since the first hominids appeared at Olduvai Gorge, to the north of present-day Tanzania. By the way, what would have become of humanity if the gorge were deeper and its edges even steeper and more difficult to cross for the descendants of [ape] Lucy? Mobility is a personal prerogative and an essential component of individuals' human capital. However, migration processes more than all other demographic phenomena and behaviours suffer the interference of organised social structures. Across a long stretch of history, the movements of humans – from short-distance movements, between one village and the next, to long-distance ones, from one end of a continent to the other or even between continents – took place in a spatial continuum. The length of the journey was proportional to the forces of push and pull that were at stake. The birth and strengthening of organised states has produced a 'spatial' discontinuity in migration processes, distinguishing between a domestic migration, which is generally free in modern countries, and international migration, which is subjected to strict limits. The exact definition of territory emerged with the modern state, through fixed, precisely drawn geographical confines and through the identification of the person who lives within these confines with the subject or the citizen.[4] The norms that allow people to cross borders and move to a foreign country and that regulate international migration flows (legal ones, of course) were consolidated. The documentation needed to cross borders was standardised, and the passport was born. Meanwhile the porous borders that had allowed free circulation between the world's countries and regions even at the beginning of the twentieth century – for example between English-speaking America and Hispanic America – disappeared forever.

The international community is now seeking new 'watchwords' and appeals to orient the line of march that governments and supranational organisations should follow in future decades. As I already discussed in Chapter 4 (and see also Chapter 8), while the demographic question was very much present in the debates of the second half of the twentieth century, it is no longer at the centre of the international agenda. Migrations are even less so – and one can understand why. While other demographic questions are mostly influenced by decisions made within states, governing migration would presuppose agreements between states and transfers of sovereignty to supranational bodies. As yet there have not been any proposals for such bodies in the international arena (or, if there were, they went unheeded). However, the two pathologies mentioned above may well become threats to the stability and sustainability that the international community pursues above all else.

I have repeatedly challenged the idea that our present era is marked by the arrival of an 'end of demography', in which the world would reach stationary population numbers and a homogenisation of demographic behaviours – including migration – across countries and continents. According to UN calculations, the net flow of migrants between the 'less developed world' and the 'more developed world' amounted to around 3.3 million a year between 2005 and 2010 and will fall to 2.2 million a year around mid-century, to 1.6 million a year in the 2070s, and to zero by 2100.[5] Each individual country's net migration flows will also have fallen heavily by the end of the century. Yet the pressures that even today drive migration flows are under considerable strain. This is true first of all of the demographic spur to migration, as the case study that compared the evolution of Germany and Nigeria clearly demonstrated in Chapter 4. Seeking to make this argument still more precise, Table 6.1 compares active-age population numbers (net of migration) in developed and developing countries between 2015 and 2050, as well as the evolution of the populations on one side and the other of

Table 6.1 Active age population (20–65 years of age, in millions) and its development, 2015–2050

	2015	2050	change %
More developed countries	758	607	–20.0
Less developed countries	3,478	4,813	+38.4
USA	192	182	–5.2
Mexico	72	99	+37.5
Italy	35	24	–31.4
North Africa	121	203	+67.8
Japan	71	49	–31.0
Philippines	54	98	+77.8

Source: United Nations, *World Population Prospects*: The 2012 Revision. New York, 2013 (at http://esa.un.org/unpd/wpp/unpp/panel_population. htm): median variant, no migration

the line – still very clear today – that separates the rich from the poor countries: the United States and Mexico, Italy and North Africa, and Japan and the Philippines. The data do not demand much further commentary: a major rise in the poor countries (+38 per cent) corresponds to a clear decline in their richer counterparts (–20 per cent). The demographic incentive to migration thus remains a powerful force, with effects that are certainly still to be felt.[6]

There also remains a strong economic incentive, which results from differentials in living standards and feeds pressures to migrate from poor countries to rich ones. During the nineteenth and twentieth centuries the inequalities between countries (measured in terms of income per capita) increased; this tendency was reversed in the 1990s, first on account of the rapid growth of numerous once very poor countries (including China and later India) and, in recent years, on account of a crisis that primarily hit the rich world. Notwithstanding this reversal, inequalities – and, together with them, incentives to migration – remain very strong. Reducing them is dependent either on continual and rapid growth in the poor countries, or, alternatively, on projects for redistributing wealth from richer to poorer countries. This first solution can only take place over the (very) long term; the second is even more remote, if we think – for example – of the very miserly levels of the Official Development Assistance (ODA), which today stand at historic lows. There is, however, also a 'third way to reduce inequality and poverty' worldwide 'by way of migration'. Let me take the liberty of reproducing a long passage, which explains the question at the heart of this chapter in a particularly incisive way:

> Migration is likely to become one of the key problems – or solutions, depending on one's viewpoint – of the 21st century. To give just one stark example: if you classify countries, by their GDP per capita level, into four 'worlds', going from the rich world of advanced nations, with GDPs per capita of over $20,000 per year, to the poorest, fourth, world with incomes under $1,000 per year, there are 7 points in the world where rich and poor countries are geographically closest to each other, whether it is because they share a border, or because the sea distance between them is minimal. You would not be surprised to find out that all these 7 points have mines, boat patrols, walls and fences to prevent free movement of people. The rich world is fencing itself in, or fencing others out. But the pressures of migration are remaining strong, despite the current crisis, simply because the differences in income levels are so huge. I conclude with something that resembles a slogan: either poor countries will become richer, or poor people will move to rich countries. Actually, these two developments can be seen as equivalent. Development is about people: either poor people have ways to become richer where they are now, or they can become rich by moving somewhere else.

These are the words not of an activist, but of a scholar who is also a top functionary in an international organisation.[7] This was a consideration John Kenneth Galbraith already offered some decades ago, defining migration as the surest route out of poverty, in a positive-sum game for the countries of departure, the countries of arrival, and the migrants themselves.[8] Moreover, the great transatlantic migration of the nineteenth and early twentieth centuries was an important factor in the globalisation process that reduced the inequalities between Europe and America.

Table 6.2 shows the average GDP of three rich and seven poor countries in 1950, 1980, and 2013.[9] Figures are given in 'international dollars', adjusted for purchasing power. Deliberately summary in nature, these data show that there

Table 6.2 GDP per capita, in international dollars, in rich and poor countries, 1950, 1980 and 2013

Year	Average: 3 rich countries	Average: 7 poor countries	Relative difference	Absolute difference
1950	$10,284	$793	×13.0	$9.491
1980	$27,230	$1,906	×14.3	$25.324
2013	$47,389	$7,831	×6.1	$39.558

Sources: United Nations, World Bank
Note: 3 rich countries: USA, Germany, Japan; 7 poor countries: China, India, Indonesia, Nigeria, South Africa, Mexico, Brazil. Averages weighted by population.

is still a very great disproportion between per capita income in rich and in poor countries. While the relative difference changes little over the first three decades, it decreases heavily in the following thirty-three years. In absolute terms, the difference increases enormously – quadrupling between 1950 and 2013 – thus massively widening the purchasing power divide between the citizens of the two halves of the world.

I thus return to the points made at the beginning of this chapter. The demographic and economic incentives to migration remain an enduring and powerful force, and so will they continue to be. The more prosperous countries are closing in on themselves. Borders are being strengthened. Migrant tragedies continue, at sea and on land alike. The international community seems impotent to intervene.

We should not be surprised that borders are being strengthened, in many cases militarised, or even made uncrossable. In the abstract it is wholly legitimate for a state to want to block irregular migration flows, human trafficking, and infiltration by criminals or terrorists. However, there can be no justification for borders to remain blocked to those who seek asylum and international protection – and this is indeed the case in many parts of the world. A secure border is also a guarantee and a condition of a country's ability to implement its own migration policy without its being shaped by irregular migration flows. If anything, the problem lies in these policies' lack of coherence. But that is another question.

While strong demographic, social, and economic inequalities persist in spite of globalisation, thus keeping up the pressures that encourage migration, immigration policies in the rich countries have become more restrictive. This tendency clearly came into view in the early part of the twenty-first century and was then strengthened in the years of crisis. This is such a complex subject that here I can only mark out some of its basic contours. Some countries are trying to restrict migration flows, making downward revisions of the 'quota' (or number) of migrants they will take in. As for the influx of workers, they are adopting admission criteria that encourage more skilled migrants and those with greater human capital. It is for this reason that we are seeing the spread of 'points system' policies assigning each candidate for migration a score based on objective criteria like age, education, knowledge of languages, skills, and profession. The points scale is then used to select which migrants will be accepted. It is being made easier for foreign investors and rentiers to move in and for foreign students to settle, even after having finished their studies.[10] Conversely, where the recruitment of the general or seasonal workforce is concerned, the tendency is to adopt more specific, more rigorous criteria. These measures are inconsistent with the continuing demand for generic labour even in the most advanced economies. There are also restrictive measures concerning family reunions, which in many countries represent the predominant means of immigration. Taken together, these measures form a kaleidoscope that shifts in the direction of greater selection and more rigorous controls.

It may well be that a generalised, stable recovery could alter or correct the tendency towards greater restrictions on migration that is now taking hold in the rich countries. However, other factors will hinder or delay any such sea change. Never in the history of the last two centuries has the migration question been weighed by political meaning as much as in the early days of this century. The discussion over what policies should be adopted and followed is overlaid with concerns over identity, nativist movements, xenophobic and racist impulses, as well as with the objective difficulties of painlessly integrating high numbers of migrants – who are almost always the bearers of different cultures – into affluent and often rather sclerotic societies.

Recent history offers some indicators that might help us to understand the possible future developments of phenomena related to migration. First of all, we should note that this is a phenomenon that mostly concerns the developed world. Today the total international migrant stock is close to a quarter of a billion (244 million in 2015), but this happens mostly in the rich world. While the rich regions account for but a fifth of the global population, they take in almost six tenths of the total migrant stock (in 1960 it was little more than four tenths). Table 6.3 provides some aggregate data. It is first of all worth noting that the proportion of migrants as a share of total population has tripled in the rich world (from 34 per 1,000 in 1960 to 108 per 1,000 in 2013), while it has fallen by 5 per cent in the poor world, where it represents only a small fraction of the size. The annual net flow of people from poor to rich countries amounted to 0.6 million in the 1960s, 1.3 million in the 1970s, 1.5 million in the 1980s, 2.8 million in the 1990s, and 3.5 million in the first

Table 6.3   International migrant stock 1960–2013 (people born abroad and residents of foreign nationality)

	World	Developed countries	Less developed countries
(Millions of people)			
1960	75.5	32.3	43.2
1980	99.3	47.5	51.8
2000	174.5	103.4	71.1
2013	231.5	135.6	95.9
(Per 1,000 inhabitants)			
1960	25.0	34.0	20.8
1980	22.4	41.7	15.7
2000	28.5	86.7	14.4
2013	32.3	108.2	16.2

Source: United Nations, *Trends in International Migrant Stock: The 2013 Revision*. DESA, Population Division (United Nations database, POP/DB/ MIG/Stock/Rev.2013/Origin), 2013, at http://www.un.org/en/development/ desa/population/publications/pdf/migration/migrant-stock-origin-2013.pdf.

decade of the twenty-first century. In this last decade Europe
overtook North America as the main destination for migrants.
As I discussed in Chapter 3, in the rich countries immigration
constitutes by now a major, structural element of the turnover
in the make-up of society.

Another aspect of great future importance is the fact that
an ever smaller number of countries remain 'excluded from'
the global migration system. This is the logical consequence
of expanding international mobility, lowered travel costs,
accessibility of information, and the possibility of getting to
know the destination country 'virtually'. But it is also the
consequence of higher education levels and of a growing
number of people's capacity to 'invest' in migration as a
strategy – this being a strategy that remains closed to the
masses of people trapped in poverty and underdevelopment.
In short, a growing proportion of the world's population –
which is itself growing – is able to plan and eventually go
through with migration strategies. We might for example
think of the sub-Saharan populations that were once absent
from migration flows on account of their isolation and
extreme poverty, and yet are today the protagonists of considerable population movements. We should also consider the
fact that some big emerging countries are now themselves
becoming central to new migration systems: South Africa as
a destination for migrants from other sub-Saharan countries,
Brazil for other South American ones, and Thailand for Cambodia and Myanmar. And we can presume that economic
growth differentials between regions and countries in the
Global South may also bring about new and different migration flows in future.

The history of the modern world is intersected by a series
of waves of globalisation. Here I ascribe this term a wider
meaning than the commonplace one, which refers to the
interconnection of economies through finance, trade, and the
movement of workers. Globalisation also means interaction
in other spheres, be they scientific, cultural, social, political,
or religious; it is plural and dynamic and has undergone
phases of acceleration, stagnation, and recession. When globalisation is strengthened, the opportunities for exchange –
including the exchange of people – between the different
regions of the world increase and the transmission of impulses

between them becomes more powerful. The world may well be embarking on a fourth phase of globalisation, which will be different from the three previous ones, most importantly in that it is increasingly dematerialised.

The first modern wave of globalisation was the one that involved Europe and America. By the mid-sixteenth century the greater part of the American continent had been explored; by 1570 it had a population of between 150,000 and 200,000 Spanish and Portuguese people; each year dozens and dozens of ships cut across the Atlantic loaded with people, animals, plants, seeds, tools, manufactured goods, silver, and gold; and there also began an intensive traffic in slaves between Africa and America. With the foundation of Manila in 1571, regular shipping between Mexico and the Philippines, and the export of silver to China to buy precious commodities for European markets, this first globalisation process also extended to Asia.

The second wave of globalisation took off around the middle of the nineteenth century. The processes of international economic integration sharply accelerated and became increasingly geographically extensive. Exports grew everywhere, rather more rapidly than production itself. In the words of Angus Maddison, the 1870–1913 period

> was an era of improved communications and substantial factor mobility. There was a massive flow of foreign capital, particularly from the UK which directed about half its savings abroad. French and German investment were also very substantial, and there were significant flows from the USA and other countries. British foreign assets were equivalent to one and a half times its GDP, French assets about fifteen percent more than GDP, German assets about 40 per cent.[11]

Nineteenth-century economic integration profoundly impacted migration, as wide layers of the European population became available for emigration. This was especially true of the continent's rural population, through the acceleration of demographic growth, increased agricultural productivity, the rise of mass unemployment and underemployment in the countryside, the great improvement of transport networks and lowering of transport costs, and the reduction of the barriers to emigration. All this took place in parallel with the rising demand for labour power in the countries of the Americas, which were rich in both land and the capital profitably invested by the European countries themselves, but poor in the workforce so abundant in small and densely populated Europe. Emigration was thus an integral part of the globalisation process, which – among other things – determined a certain convergence in real wages between Europe and America, and indeed in the relative prices of other factors of production and land rents – land having earlier been cheap and abundant in America and scarce and expensive in Europe.[12]

Internationalisation processes took off again in the wake of the Second World War. Between 1960 and 2010 the exports of goods and services grew much more quickly than the GDP, bearing witness to the tightening of international links. International trade was worth 12.7 per cent of the world GDP in 1970 and 30 per cent by 2013. In this historical period there have been multiple and pervasive links between globalisation and migration. But one of the main characteristics of this phase is the divergence in states' and international institutions' policies regarding the international exchange of the factors of production. One the one hand, there has been a sustained push to reduce tariff barriers and customs controls on cash flows and on the flows of goods and services, through the creation of a powerful supranational regulatory body: the World Trade Organisation (WTO). On the other hand, strong controls on migrant movements have persisted, and indeed there is a tendency further to strengthen restrictions in this area. The weakening convergence of economic conditions in countries of origin and of destination – contrary to what happened in the previous cycle of globalisation between Europe and America – is due to this policy divergence.

The third globalisation process has slowed the drive towards migration through the long economic crisis that began in 2008. It may slowly be changing face, turning into a fourth wave of internationalisation, able to replace the one that is already under way. Three tendencies are currently taking root and have long-term effects that are difficult to evaluate from today's standpoint. The first consists of the slow mutation of the traditional forms of migration, which had entailed a sharp distinction between long-term migration, where migrants put down roots; short-term migration, where they had solid plans to return to their homeland; migration of the seasonal type; and migration for other reasons (education, healthcare, religion). These forms of migration differed also in terms of the varying degrees to which they involved other parts of the family unit. The second tendency concerns a growing process of ethnic mixing, which tends to create diffuse and robust links between communities that live in different countries. The third tendency is more evanescent and concerns the spread of various forms of contact between populations, above and beyond – and despite the borders that divide the states.

The first of these tendencies is clearly reflected in the continual alteration and adaptation of the norms governing migration. Migration for work reasons is (in theory) regulated on the basis of market needs. These needs, however, shift rapidly, which makes the original decisions obsolete. Spouses or children reunited with the migrant end up entering the labour market too, even if they arrived as family members; those who arrive for reasons of study try to find work after finishing their courses; seasonal workers repeat their migrant journey each year and seek means to establish themselves; migrants arriving as part of circular migration schemes[13] want to sink roots in the host country, whereas other migrants, who arrived with the intention of putting down roots, opt instead for returning to their homelands. Naturally, these shifts are as old as migration itself. But today they are becoming much more frequent, and even normal rather than occasional. The complexity and mobility of contemporary societies is the cause of this change.

The second tendency concerns the growth of interethnic marriages (and the births that result). It implicates all those societies that are – or have been – destination countries for migration. Naturally there are certain eras and societies in which these phenomena are much more intense. Between 1538 and 1547, at Lima Cathedral (opened for worship in 1535, two years after the killing of Atahualpa), some 347 out of the 853 babies baptised were the children of an indigenous woman and a Spanish man![14] But things were very different in the western world: one should bear in mind the United States, where the last state laws banning interracial marriage were abolished only in 1967, through the Supreme Court case *Loving v Virginia*. Unfortunately, important though this phenomenon is, there is a lack of satisfactory data about it, so the little that does exist will have to do. An estimated 15 per cent of the new marriages in the United States in 2010 crossed different ethnic or racial groups; this percentage almost doubled the 8 per cent figure for existing marriages as a whole (regardless of the wedding date). Public opinion surveys also show that the percentage of Americans who disapproved of mixed marriages has fallen in the past half-century from over 90 per cent to less than 20 per cent. In France one in four weddings involves a foreign spouse; the figure for England and Wales is one in five, for Spain, one in seven, and, for Italy, one in nine. One cross-Europe comparative study based on samples of the workforce in various countries measured the proportion of mixed couples (with one spouse born abroad) in all married couples, in thirty countries, over the 2005–7 and 2008–10 periods. One in ten were mixed couples, and there were percentages close to zero in Romania and over 20 per cent in Switzerland and Latvia.[15] It would be interesting to follow how this phenomenon develops in future in terms of mixed couples, their offspring, and their respective choices of partnering and reproduction. However, these are also rising phenomena that have a tendency to create new links between ethnicities and countries.

The third tendency is a more complex and articulated one, and no metric has yet been identified for evaluating its overall strength. This tendency concerns the intensification of relations among individuals who do not join migration flows (or cannot do so) but generate international bonds of affection, friendship, employment, or even simple knowledge of a given country. This category would include, for example, visits for travel or tourism: in 1950 so-called 'international' tourists were 25 million in number, but by 2013 the figure had risen to 1.1 billion, and in 2030 it is predicted to hit 1.8 billion.[16] In 1990 little more than 1 million Chinese people travelled outside of their country for work or tourism, whereas in 2013 the number was close to 100 million. Of course, the contacts made through tourism or work and business trips are rather superficial; but they certainly do create a thick web of relations, if not bonds. The reciprocal knowledge deriving from exchanges for study is at a whole different level, and so-called 'international students' have enormously increased in number over time. In 1990 there were 1.3 million university-level international students in the Organisation for Economic Co-Operation and Development (OECD) countries, and 4.3 million in 2011. There has also been a stunning explosion in virtual means of communication: the most recent edition (2015) of the Internet statistical bible informs us that 3 billion people (41 per cent of the world population) are active Internet users, 2.1 billion (29 per cent) subscribed to social media, and 3.6 billion (51 per cent) have a mobile phone.[17] The numbers continue to increase. It is no exaggeration to speak of an 'explosion', if we consider that twenty years ago almost none of this existed. It has been written that 'every time someone moves to another country their family and friends in the origin gain a piece of social capital in the destination and a network is established along which money, information, ideas and more migrants flow'.[18]

Here, then, is the fourth era of globalisation. We face a future where the unknown variable is the extent of the real migration flows caught between the binds of the state and the continual tension of push and pull factors; where what we do know for certain is that exchanges between people – mostly online – will be ever more intensive. Once reliant just on the written word, today these exchanges are instantly carried by words, voices and images.

How 'politically' sustainable can this multiform, inevitably expanding phenomenon be, in a planetary space that is more and more restricted and interconnected? In general, international institutions 'sweep this problem under the carpet', limiting themselves to invoking respect for human rights and for international conventions. Even initiatives of modest scope aimed at the governance or coordination of migration are in general reduced to declarations of intent. In free-trade areas such as the North Atlantic Free Trade Agreement (NAFTA, between Canada, the United States, and Mexico) or Mercosur (between Argentina, Brazil, Paraguay, Uruguay, Venezuela), migration flows are still a national prerogative. And, while the European Union has common policies for visas, borders, integration, and refusal of entry, each state maintains exclusive prerogatives over admission policies, including the number of migrants it will receive. The reality is that no country is prepared to cede even a slight fraction of its own sovereignty to any kind of supranational institution with even minimal normative powers. Thus migration – especially long-term migration that involves an enduring or permanent relocation from one country to another – remains subjected to the power of demographic, economic, and social inequalities; to the efficiency of the channels and barriers regulating the influx into each individual destination country; and to how watertight the policies of each exit country are. Migrants' rights often prove to be no more than a piece of paper, as they are crushed between the powerful interests of the countries of departure and those of arrival.

If even minimal proposals for governing or coordinating migration have been derailed, what can we say of the idea of gradually creating a WTO-style organisation to which states would cede some share of their sovereignty (even a minimal amount, in the initial phases) over questions related to migration? Proposals of this nature do not seem popular in the international debate and are left to isolated voices. I can leave aside the complex juridical and international question of the kind of institution that ought to be invested with the powers to regulate migration: that is, the question of whether it ought to be a new and autonomous agency, like a world migration organisation, or a fusion of existing agencies – for instance the United Nations High Commissioner for Refugees (UNHCR) and the International Organization for Migration (IOM); whether it should be external or internal to the UN family; and so on. Let us think instead about the roles that such an agency could take on. In the initial phase it could focus on useful and politically uncontroversial tasks, or at least on only moderately controversial ones – for example, the fields of information and data collection and analysis of migration trends; policy analysis and the study of proposals for further policy development; technical assistance, education, provision of certain services, and constitution of an institutional forum for discussion and comparison; support for negotiations and anti-trafficking initiatives. These are relatively neutral tasks, without significant conflicts of interest, and they could constitute the initial operational basis for an international institution aimed at building cooperation among states. But other functions could also be added in successive phases, if an embryo of migration governance did develop. Think of the question of identifying migrants – certifying their place of birth, nationality, age and family situation, professional status, education level, knowledge of languages, and – if relevant – criminal records; the task of ensuring that migrants' remittances can freely circulate at minimum cost and with maximum security, that pension rights are not lost once they have been acquired, and that work contracts conform to minimum standards. Then there is the important task of promoting and maintaining (and, if necessary, guaranteeing respect for) bilateral and multilateral accords regarding family reunions or the readmission of legally expelled migrants to their own countries; also the implementation of a 'dual nationality' that should embrace both the country of origin and the country of residence, specifying the migrant's rights and duties towards each of the two; and – lastly and most importantly of all – the protection of migrants' rights: those who migrate legally, but also the tens of millions who live in foreign countries illegally. In many countries even legal migrants live in a state of semi-servitude, subjected to threats and having their passports withheld by the authorities or by employers.

All these functions would still leave the essential prerogatives regarding admission policies, integration, and expulsion in the hands of individual states, but within a framework of transparency and respect for basic rights and rules. It is an unsustainable and unacceptable paradox that the world wants a *Homo sapiens*, yes – but not one who should also be a *Homo movens*!

7

Long Lifespans
Have Their Cost

- A woman from Arles lived to 122 years of age
- In the rich countries a life expectancy of 90 is not far off
- The sustainability of long lifespans
- The profile of a 100-year-old society
- Rigid ages, flexible roles
- Four generations under one roof

In a state of nature there is 'no knowledge of the face of the earth; no account of time, no arts, no letters, no society, and, which is worst of all, continual fear and danger of violent death, and the life of man solitary, poor, nasty, brutish, and short'.[1] Perhaps these words could be considered appropriate for the short human lives of the Palaeolithic, but without doubt living conditions in contemporary societies, and especially rich ones, are very different from those portrayed by Thomas Hobbes. Lifespans are long and getting longer: reaching 100 years of age is still rare but no longer exceptional, and it is not long before we will consider it absolutely normal. Given that, in many advanced populations, women's life expectancy is approaching 90,[2] it is worth reflecting on the complex social and cultural implications that a further extension of lifespans might have. But first one should ponder what are the foundations of increased longevity and its limits, if indeed such limits exist.

Jeanne Calment, the well-to-do shopkeeper who died in Arles on 4 August 1997, did not have a 'brutish and short' life. This would not in itself be of any great interest, were it not for the fact that Jeanne was born – again, in Arles – on 21 February 1875, at a time when the wounds of the Paris Commune were still painfully unhealed, and that she was the oldest ever person whose age can be proven incontrovertibly. Of course Methuselah and other Old Testament figures are said to have lived far longer, but alas there were no records kept back then and the proofs of their age are more than a little precarious. One hundred and twenty-two years is a long lifespan, but we might think it likely to remain an exceptional case owing to an extraordinary coincidence of events, of little importance for society. But things are not quite so simple. In all countries that do have trustworthy systems of birth regis-tration, we can see that something very interesting is going on. Year after year, notwithstanding the fluctuations due to chance, the 'maximum' death age (the age of the oldest person who dies each year) has continued to move upwards. This results in part from a merely statistical phenomenon: the range of candidates has grown somewhat because many more people survive their 90s, 100s or more, and somewhat because population numbers more generally have increased. It is easier for chance to produce exceptional, record-beating cir-cumstances in a pool of 10,000 or 100,000 people than in a group of just 100. Even so, the most important factor lies in the fact that it is impossible to identify a 'limit point' of human life and that the maximum age at death shifts in rela-tion to the improvement of a population's health levels. The case of Sweden – which offers trustworthy and precise centen-nial statistics – has been studied in some detail. In the 1860s the maximum age at death fluctuated, year in year out, around 101; the figure then gradually increased, reaching 109 at the beginning of the century (around 108 for men and 110 for women). The strongest increase, however, came in the past three decades, when the maximum age at death increased at an average rate of around 1.1 years per decade. We can hypothesise that – if things continue at this pace – by the end of the century the record 'cciling' of 122 years reached by

Jeanne Calment could become the extreme limit (an oxymoron, this: the extreme 'normal' limit) of lifespan in the rich countries. The maximum lifespan is, of course, a matter related to one individual and not a significant part of the collective, and increases in such a record may not seem very important. However, this is not the case. For, together with the increase in the maximum lifespan, there is also a very strong increase in the number of people who survive into very old age – past 90 or 100, for example. In the Italian case, up until the 1950s fewer than ten out of every 10,000 newborns lived to 100 years of age, but today around 300 do so. In Japan around 1950 this figure was, like in Italy, smaller than ten per 10,000, whereas today it is higher than 600. More than one third of the babies born in Italy in 2013 will reach 90, and for a generation of women this is the single age at which deaths are most numerous (in Japan the respective figures are 47 per cent and 92 years of age).[3]

How far – and how quickly – will lifespans continue to increase? If it seems that women's average lifespans are about to reach 90 (men are a few years behind, but they, too, have made rapid advances), then what should we expect for the rest of the century? Many scholars have worked to investigate what the 'age limit' of an average lifespan might be across a general, non-selected population. This notion can serve as our guide in outlining possible future scenarios. But the extreme limits that have thus far been identified[4] have been in fact quickly surpassed by reality.

There are serious scholars who maintain that genetic, biological, medical, and pharmaceutical knowledge will in the future allow people to reach lifespans that are today unthinkable (and indeed half a century ago no one would have considered that today's levels were possible). Moreover, if we look at the risks of death at various ages (for instance at 70, 80, or 90), we see that they have decreased over time up until the present day. For instance, while in 1960 a person who reached the age of 90 had a 27 per cent probability of dying before her 91st birthday, this figure declined to 23 per cent in 1980, to 16 per cent in 2000 and to 12 per cent in 2013. There is an analogous tendency at other ages, and (for now) there are no substantial indications of a slowdown or stasis in improvements at very advanced ages.[5] It has been argued that we are not at present close to a limit point and that, if such a limit point existed, this downward tendency would slow to zero. To reduce a very complex thesis to its bare outline, the argument is that the most important life-threatening illnesses are closely dependent on risk factors that can be changed, reduced, or even eliminated, so that – given appropriate lifestyles and the very high availability of the necessary medical services, pharmaceuticals, technologies, and knowledges – this progress could continue in the long term. A life expectancy of 100 (or more) could be within populations' grasp in this century. This hypothesis is at least consistent with the longevity of certain selected groups, with impeccable lifestyles from a health point of view (good diets, physical exercise, no smoking, little alcohol, diligent medical check-ups, and excellent treatment). I can leave out of this discussion the claims made by the latest charlatans, who see lifespans of 120, 150 or more at arm's length, in general without the slightest scientific foundation.

There is, however, a different, rather more cautious line of thought, based on evolutionist reasoning. In this view, natural selection works effectively to strengthen reproduction, refining the organism's capacities to maintain and repair itself. Given favourable circumstances, everyone or almost everyone survives up to the end of the reproductive cycle (in Italy 98 per cent of newborns reach the age of 50, as against barely one third of the Italians born in the era of national unification [i.e. in the 1860s] and half of those born in 1900). Yet (again according to this argument) natural selection does not work so efficiently beyond the age of reproduction; it is as if Nature (with a capital N, as if it were an identifiable entity) had no interest in avoiding decay, old age, and death. While this theory relies more on abstract reasoning than on concrete proofs, it does have a certain logical power of its own. That said, it is also worth remembering that intergenerational cooperation is an important factor in sustaining both child and adult survival rates, and thus it is useful to the human species in general that the elderly do stay alive. Naturally, controlling the risk factors associated with various diseases has served considerably to improve survival rates among the elderly, delaying the flare-up of those illnesses proper to old age itself. However, in the meantime there has also been a growth in new or rare illnesses. Given that there is no genetic programme for a much more extended life, we can expect that the struggle against old-age illnesses will become a more difficult one, with diminishing returns as mortality rates fall. Those who follow these lines of reasoning do not rule out the possibility of further progress in human longevity, but they maintain that we are approaching its natural limits.

A more pragmatic view holds that increased longevity is due to multiple factors that act either simultaneously or in series and that none of them is decisive on its own. One can infer this much from the (almost) linear and continuous advance in life expectancy during the last century and a half among the populations with the utmost well-being. Not even revolutionary biomedical discoveries – such as the confirmation of the germ theory of infectious diseases at the end of the nineteenth century, the discovery of antibacterial drugs in the 1930s and 1940s, or the development of new treatments for cardiovascular illnesses in the last half-century – have left any visible marks of acceleration on the human lifespan. And we might presume that no fresh 'revolutionary' discovery will be able to do so in future. It is precisely because of the multiplicity of factors that contribute to greater longevity (diet, lifestyles, economic and material resources, environmental conditions, the availability of medicine, technology, access to treatment) that the experts responsible for 'predicting' the future prefer to graft extrapolatory mathematical models onto past tendencies, while also incorporating factors that slow the pace of change as mortality decreases. According to the UN forecasts repeatedly cited above, life expectancy at birth in the country with the greatest longevity, Japan, will rise from 83 (both genders) in 2013 to 89 in 2050 and to 94 in 2100, as the rate of increase slows.[6]

But if the population is living to increasingly higher ages, how will it live the extra years thus 'gained', so far as health is concerned? Up until – and even beyond – the mid-twentieth century, life expectancy gains came as the consequence of higher survival rates, in infancy as well as among young people and adults. This mostly meant people being saved from infectious diseases and resuming wholly normal lives after they had been treated. Conversely, the massive gains in life expectancy from the 1960s onwards have almost exclusively come from improving survival rates at old and very old ages. Nonetheless, one question remains open: how good is the quality of life in the extra years that have been gained, or in those – not a few – that will be gained in future? Answering this question is crucial if longevity is to be socially and economically sustainable. There are two opposite schools of thought in this regard, commonly referred to as 'compression' and 'expansion' theories of illness. According to the former, longevity is close to its limits and medical progress and good behaviour tend to delay the flare-up of illnesses, 'compressing' them into a person's final years. According to the 'expansion' theory, medical progress allows a growing proportion of fragile individuals to reach very old ages and survive even in the presence of debilitating diseases (for example senile dementia). The evidence collected thus far, most of it based on the results of studies into people's perceptions of their own health, would seem to lean towards the 'compression' theory. But there is still not enough unequivocal proof, and this therefore remains an open question. Evidently, if the 'compression' theory were proven correct, old people's better overall health would wholly or partly compensate for the greater burden that derives from their growing weight among the overall population. This would be crucial for the sustainability of longevity as well as for society's general well-being.

Substantial progress is therefore possible, so long as the conditions underpinning current predictions do indeed come to pass, in other words in conditions of social and economic stability, reasonable economic growth, and further scientific advances that can be transferred to the practical plane. But if the '100-year society' is a theoretically possible future, is it also a plausible one? And can we take it for granted that the long life that is today the prerogative of the most advanced countries will be 'sustainable'? What difficulties, what obstacles, what adaptations will it be necessary to address in order to maintain and improve the survival levels that have already been reached? These questions need weighing up in biological, social, economic, and, finally, political terms. In any case, these terms do not constitute clearly distinct or independent aspects, for they also interact among themselves.

THE BIOLOGICAL ASPECT   The most advanced countries have proven themselves able to address the changeability of the world of diseases, an instability that derives from the complex interrelation between microbes, carriers, the environment, and individual people. The new diseases that have emerged in recent decades – SARS, Ebola, Lyme disease, legionella, Hepatitis C, and BSE (or mad cow disease) – have had little impact, and even the most serious one – HIV/AIDS – has been combated successfully. Prevention systems have been strengthened and the means of treatment have become more effective.

THE SOCIAL ASPECT   Diseases of a mainly social origin are much more dangerous, including those linked to the abuse of drugs, alcohol, and smoking; those linked to diet, such as obesity and its cardiovascular and diabetic sequelae; or illnesses and syndromes of a neurological character, such as depression. Smoking – certainly the habit most damaging to health – is in decline almost everywhere in the advanced world. Well-organised and socially stable countries with well-educated populations do seem able to control and reduce illnesses linked to individual behaviour.

THE ECONOMIC ASPECT   The longevity that the world's most fortunate countries can boast is in good measure based on their modern, efficient, universal-access healthcare systems. We find further proof of this in the rapid improvement in recent immigrants' survival rates, visible in numerous cases. Even though they bring with them the customs and habits, lifestyles and consumption patterns proper to their countries of origin, they enjoy the healthcare systems of the arrival countries. If we were to close down our hospitals, clinics, and medical facilities, we would turn back to the survival levels of 100 years ago – even if this would not plunge us back into the natural state described by Hobbes. However, healthcare systems cost money and, under pressure from a rapidly aging population, over time, their cost has increased more quickly than price levels in general. Between 1990 and 2010 healthcare spending rose from 6.8 per cent to 9.4 per cent of the GDP in the Organisation for Economic Co-Operation and Development (OECD) countries; it rose from 12.4 per cent to 17.7 per cent of the GDP in the United States, from 8.3 per cent to

11.6 per cent in France and Germany, and from 7.7 to 9.4 per cent in Italy. In these recent years of crisis this growth has been interrupted, also on account of the heavy cuts in public spending.

Various factors are contributing to this tendency for healthcare spending to become an increasingly large proportion of the GDP, in the first place the fact that old people – who require more intensive health and medical treatment – make up an increasingly large part of the population. However, the rising costs of providing treatments with a high technological content – with prices rising faster than those in other sectors of the economy – are also a contributing factor. Moreover, if, as many people fear, extended lifespans do entail the emergence of diseases linked to old age and determine an increase in years lived in good health that is less than proportionate to the increase in years lived in precarious health, then this would add a factor of extra cost to the ones mentioned above. We should thus ask ourselves what the sustainable limits to the growth in healthcare spending would be; whether healthcare, through its competition for income with other possible recipients (education, security, welfare, the environment), does not risk soon reaching the limits of its expansion; and, finally, whether any such limits as are introduced do not imply limits to the expansion of survival rates and do not threaten the levels that have already been reached.

THE POLITICAL ASPECT Social organisation depends on policy choices, in particular those that involve the distribution of resources. As I said above, here the hypothesis is political stability, so I will leave aside the profound upheavals caused by revolutions or sudden transformations, such as those that struck the Soviet Union and its empire in the 1980s and 1990s, turning back the clock on healthcare and survival rates by decades. I will suppose that some of the tendencies that are already emerging are going to become more powerful and that, faced with the lack of public funds, some of the expense in healthcare is going to be shifted onto the users' own shoulders, making them contribute to the cost of check-ups, treatment, medicine, and hospital stays. How serious the consequences will be depends on the intensity of the changes. Some layers of the population may go without healthcare services and treatments, inequalities between citizens may increase, and improvements in survival rates may come to a halt or be reversed among more or less circumscribed groups.

The conclusion is that the long lifespans in modern states are underpinned by a delicate balance of actions and forces that are biological, social, economic, and political in nature and that this balance can be maintained and strengthened but also compromised by unexpected events, mistaken actions, and social inertia.

Let us now suppose that the transition to the 100-year society were already complete and that the situation had been 'stabilised' – a demographic expression with an intuitively clear meaning. Let us consider the simplest of cases, where the population is stationary (it remains of constant size); births equal deaths; life expectancy is 100; and the maximum age at death is over 120.[7] Survival rates have reached their maximum extension and the risk of death at different ages is marked along a fixed curve. In such a situation the population structure by age would also remain constant over time. This scenario implies birth numbers equal to the replacement fertility rate of just over two children per woman, which is already the case in the United States, France, and some North European countries but not in Japan, Russia, Germany, Italy, or Spain, which remain well below this level. In many respects the 100-year society is very different from our present one.

However, many of the differences are developing gradually and could easily be absorbed by the adaptation mechanisms typical of human societies. Table 7.1 presents four age structures that correspond to stationary populations with a life expectancy of 40 (reached by the Italian population in 1895), 60 and 80 (reached in 1947 and 2002 respectively), and 100 years (which the rich countries *could* reach at the beginning of the next century).

As one can see, the series shows an age structure that shifts towards the higher ages as life expectancy increases. However, as one moves from the '80 years' column to the '100 years' column, there is a real discontinuity in the 'dimensions' of the population over 80 years of age – an easily neglected

Table 7.1 Age structure for stationary populations with life expectancies of 40, 60, 80, and 100 years

Age	40	60	80	100
0–19	35.7	29.8	24.6	19.8
20–39	29.9	27.9	24.3	19.8
40–59	22.6	24.6	23.9	19.6
60–79	11	15.7	20.5	19.2
80–99	0.5	2	6.6	16.8
100+	0	0	0.2	4.8
Total	100%	100%	100%	100%

Source: United Nations, *World Population Prospects: The 2012 Revision.* New York, 2013 (at http://esa.un.org/unpd/wpp/unpp/panel_population.htm)

fraction (2 per cent) when life expectancy is at 60 and still modest (under 7 per cent) when it reaches 80, but very considerable (16.8 per cent) in the 100 year society. For the other ages the change in the structure is more gradual, with consequences that could be managed by society's ability to adapt.

Deeper reflection shows that the structural changes apparent in the 100-year society present novel aspects by comparison to the societies that went before. A first aspect worth considering concerns the evolution of human capital – or, better, its biodemographic component. Human capital is not only the provision of knowledge and capacities acquired through education, training, or experience, but also the ability to survive and live in good health, to reproduce, and to enjoy sufficient geographic and social mobility for seeking better working and living conditions. Let's take the example of good health (an essential part, indeed the essential basis of human capital). It improved enormously over the last century through the elimination of early deaths, the reduction of disabilities, and improvements in health and physical fitness. In short, people with good demographic prerogatives were 'saved', and in the coming decades very old people with rather weaker such prerogatives will also be 'rescued'. We might say that, while over the last century (or the greater part of it) the lengthening of lifespans has had increasing returns in terms of improving human capital, as this century continues this situation may well be replaced by one of diminishing returns.

In human societies we are born helpless, growth takes place slowly, and physical decline is a prolonged process. The cycle of life is essentially made up of three phases. In the first of these phases – the phase of growth, education, and the slow process of achieving greater freedom and autonomy – we are net recipients of resources, predominantly transferred from the family. In the second phase, approximately coinciding with the active, productive life, we are net contributors – mainly making transfers to children, the community, and, if relevant, state bodies – with regard to the benefits we receive. In the third phase, retirement, we are once again net recipients. In our own time this takes place through state transfer of resources for social security, assistance, and health-care services, whereas in agricultural societies it operates through the support offered by one's descendants or the community to which one belongs. Across history these phases have varied in duration according to the length of lifespans and to particular societies' own characteristics. They have never been rigidly separate, and the functions assigned to them overlap – one may think, for example, of education for the active-age population, people retiring before they get old, or the elderly still in work. Even so, in industrial and postindustrial societies – with the various forms the welfare state has assumed over the last century and a half – these three phases have become more sharply defined, through specific age limits assigned to them. Longer lifespans have brought a redivision of these boundaries, roughly assigning one quarter of human life to the first phase, a half to the second, and the remaining quarter to the third and last phase. If this rough division of lifespans and the established norms remain the same, then the citizens of the 100-year society will have to dedicate around fifty years to work, pushing back the retirement age – which today (effectively) stands at a little above 60 – to 75 years of age. In a context of rising life expectancies and further improvements in health conditions – such as we might expect – it seems then wholly plausible (in theory) that this slippage will be complete over several decades. It does not seem in principle impossible to convince society collectively that for every extra year of life we should have to add another six months to our work careers. I do not doubt that, if people were asked to put their names to a contract of this type, the great majority of those approached would sign up without hesitation.

The rigid functional separation of age bands that has been consolidated over the last century has, however, started to dissolve. And it will continue to do so at an accelerated pace, also as a consequence of longer lifespans. Two factors seem particularly important in this regard. The first is well known and has to do with the accumulation, renewal, and updating of knowledge. Education and learning, which were once boxed into the first phase of the life cycle, are now spreading across its whole duration. This owes to the fact that societies are becoming increasingly complex; that the knowledges acquired are becoming obsolete more quickly; and that lifespans are becoming increasingly long. The second factor is different in nature and concerns the possible variation in people's health conditions, functionality, and capacities – a variability that rapidly increases as they get older. It follows that a theoretical average retirement age of 75 would imply a very wide distribution in terms of the ages at which individuals exited the productive phase: these ages would range hypothetically from 60 to 90 years. Alternatively (or in combination with this), we might expect working 'time' to vary as a function of people's ages or health conditions. One can say that societies of 100-year-olds would have to develop a great degree of flexibility in terms of how they distributed roles and functions across the different ages. And we can expect that societies unable to develop such flexibility would become burdened with serious disruption and inefficiency.

The life cycle has other rhythms, first of all the one determined by the reproductive cycle. Notwithstanding the major fall in birth rates over the last century, parents' average age at childbirth has remained around 30, without too much variation. At the beginning of the twentieth century, when birth control was still the prerogative of a minority, the greater part of the reproductive stage of life (roughly 20 to 40 years of age) was used intensively. Today, however, a few years on either side of 30 suffice for bringing a first and a second child into the world; and these, together, represent over 90 per cent of births in countries with a low birth rate. Yet the length of each generation – the average age gap between parents and children – has remained unchanged over time. It is impossible to tamper with or trick the biological clock; and, since this imposes a clear limit on women's capacity to reproduce, we can rule out the possibility that the length of each generation would increase in future. (Indeed, many quite justifiably maintain that today's 'delay' in bringing a first child into the world borders on health risk and that it would therefore be easier to reduce rather than extend it.) It is unlikely that tricking or tampering with the biological clock (which may become possible as technology develops) will become commonplace, or that reproducing at ages at which it is today impossible is going to become a mass phenomenon.

So here we have another fundamental change: in a 100-year society the coexistence of four generations will become 'normal'. There could be a close to 70 per cent probability of surviving to 90 and a near-certain chance of having children, grandchildren, and great-grandchildren (if they are born in time). Almost all grandparents would also be sons and daughters, adult men and women would have living grandparents, and in a good number of cases it would even be possible for five generations to live at once. We will leave it up to other people with richer imaginations to think through what changes this might entail for family and social relations, the transmission of experience and knowledge, the relations and hierarchies between age groups, and the transfer of wealth and assets from generation to generation.[8]

The 100-year society is a low-turnover society. Even if life expectancy is stationary at 100, comparing this situation to that of a society where life expectancy is stationary at the age of 40 is like standing in front of two lakes of the same size, the first one fed and drained by a stream and the second by a great river. The water level in the two lakes is constant, but in the first case the water is replaced very slowly and in the second case very rapidly. Naturally slow turnover – that is, long life – is what we want, and thus this marks an advance. But it also has social repercussions. Many argue that longer lifespans are 'neutral' (all other conditions being equal: in this chapter I have assumed stationary societies with neither increasing nor falling population numbers) and that they imply only a change of degree, 'pushing' the life cycle further forward. It is commonly observed that today's 70- or

80-year-old who plays sports, travels, participates in activities, and is physically well resembles the 50- or 60-year-old of half a century ago. Resembles – but is not the same. The lengthening of lifespans is certainly 'non-neutral', if for no other reason than that youth and the fullness of life – definitively left behind with the end of the reproduction period – become a gradually shorter portion of the overall life cycle. And old age is not simply a function of health and physical well-being, but also a function of the distance that gradually comes to separate it from these earlier stages.

8

Few Prescriptions for Many Ills

◆ Poverty and hunger: The millennium development goals
reached

◆ But the numbers of poor and hungry in Africa increase

◆ The burden of 168 objectives

◆ The Malthusian trap

◆ Nuclear-armed India with one in five children wasted

◆ Political mission: Concentrate efforts, dismantle the trap

The solemn Millennium Declaration by heads of states and
governments was approved by the UN General Assembly on
8 September 2000. After the usual introduction regarding the
values and principles that had inspired the international community's actions, it continued: 'We will spare no effort to free
our fellow men, women and children from the abject and
dehumanizing conditions of extreme poverty, to which more
than a billion of them are currently subjected.'[1] The first of
the eight millennium development goals, the numerical trans-
lation of this commitment, aimed to reduce the number of
people in a state of 'extreme poverty' to half of 1990 levels
by 2015. This objective was achieved: already in 2010 it was
estimated that the proportion of the world population that
found itself in such an abject situation had fallen from 36 per
cent two decades before to 18 per cent. However, between

the two dates, the world population rose 30 per cent; hence, rather than halving, the total number of people in extreme poverty fell by 37 per cent, from 1.9 to 1.2 billion. The first objective was combined with two other commitments, also supposed to be fulfilled by 2015: to halve the percentage of people suffering from hunger (by comparison to 1990) and to halve the percentage of people unable to access drinking water. 'Suffering from hunger' is a generic and subjective expression, and it was later replaced by the term 'undernourished' – a definition well-suited to biometric-type measurements. This goal, too, may well be reached by 2015: the figures for 2011–13 estimate the proportion of the world population going hungry at 14.3 per cent (1 billion), as against 23.6 per cent (1.3 billion) for 1990–2. By the by, one may note that the poor and hungry belong to two largely overlapping collectivities: they are above all concentrated in sub-Saharan Africa and south Asia; and they suffer a large share of the conditions of deprivation and underdevelopment that the millennium development goals proposed to eradicate or strongly erode, from illiteracy to gender inequalities, infectious diseases, mortality (particularly among mothers and infants), and environmental degradation.

Before proceeding, I ought to advance both an empirical and a theoretical consideration. The empirical consideration is that, even if the millennium goals on poverty and hunger are reached or almost reached, this will be true only at a planetary level, and not for the two vast regions mentioned above. In sub-Saharan Africa extreme poverty struck 48 per cent of the population in 2010, as against 56 per cent in 1990. However, during those two decades the absolute number of poor people rose by 46 per cent, to 125 million, as a result of unrestrained demographic growth. In other words, a traveller journeying up and down and across the African continent in 2010 would have met half as many poor people along the way, by comparison to a similar journey twenty years earlier. One could make a similar argument with regard to undernourishment: while its relative impact has decreased, the absolute numbers of undernourished people have increased by over 50 million (+32 per cent).

Let's go back two centuries, to the time when the world population was around 1 billion. The world population at that time was thus more or less the same as the number of people going hungry today. But not all the people in those times were suffering from hunger: the populations of the Americas and a good part of the populations of Africa had modest but adequate diets for the most part. The same could be said of the densely settled populations of Europe, which had sufficient food in normal times, even though they also suffered recurrent shortages. Without doubt, the bulk of those going hungry was found in Asia, a continent that was home to two thirds of the world's population at that time. So one could venture that two centuries ago between a third and half of the world population suffered from hunger and that the billion going hungry today are double or triple the number they were at the dawn of the Industrial Revolution. How should we judge a development process that has multipled the world population's economic means per capita tenfold, the population sevenfold, and the numbers of the destitute two- or threefold? How come a tenfold increase in GDP has not succeeded in containing or reducing the numbers of the needy? We could endlessly discuss the whys and wherefores of this, with different or opposite interpretative schemata. What we cannot do is collapse the phenomena of change into any one dimension, as we do when we welcome a reduction in the relative effect of any one unpleasant phenomenon while passing over in silence the increasing number of people who are suffering from it.

In Chapter 4 I discussed the international community's search for watchwords that might build a broad consensus for a salutary joint action. Such watchwords were found through the different declinations of the concept of sustainable development. This is a concept first elaborated in the natural sciences, and only with some simplification and strained logic can it be extended to human societies. I also noted that demographic phenomena, and in particular population growth, have been left in the background, almost as if they had become less important and were not an obstacle to achieving sustainability. Many pages of this book are dedicated to showing that the opposite is the case. Now we need to pick up on this argument again, for in September 2015 the United Nations brought the international community together for a summit to adopt a Post-2015 Development Agenda. Its intention was to mobilise the planet's political, cultural, and financial powers to promote this agenda's goals.[2] The 2000 Millennium Declaration consisted of eight general goals and sixteen concrete, quantifiable objectives, all of them clearly of great importance to development. This was a clear and verifiable 'dashboard' of indicators. The 'offspring' of the 2015 summit show how much more prolific it was than its predecessor: the preparatory documents (later adopted with minor changes) indicated that there would be seventeen sustainable development goals (SDG) with a total of 169 objectives measured by 302 indicators (experts considered many of them patently impossible to calculate).[3] They ranged from the science fictional (17.19.2, indicator of gross national happiness) to the obviously irrelevant (4.7.2, indicator of the percentage of 13-year-old pupils who support values and attitudes that promote equality, trust, and participation in government activities).[4] It is truly doubtful that such a wide array of objectives, lacking any prioritisation and ranging from the irrelevant to the evanescent, can be condensed into rationales, watchwords, and guidelines able to mobilise awareness, resources, and actions. Unfortunately, this jumble is a reflection of the international institutions' bureaucratic procedures, showing their openness to stakeholders' specific requirements but without selecting between them or ordering them by priority. While the agenda's goals touch on the themes of poverty (goal 1), nutrition (goal 2), and health and survival (goal 3), as a whole they make only indirect reference to the theme of family planning (objective 5.6, to ensure universal access to sexual and reproductive health). The document does not, however, have any orientation with regard to the pace of demographic change, family, and associative forms, the modalities of human settlement (except large-scale urbanisation), domestic mobility, or, most importantly, international migration. It confirms what we have already noted: namely that it seems that the official international community now sees demography as irrelevant to sustainable development, notwithstanding all the evidence to the contrary.

At the outset (in Chapter 1) I spoke of the transition–revolution that has allowed humanity to free itself from the conditions imposed by our environment, biology, and instincts and to adopt criteria for choosing our own reproductive and survival behaviours. Yet this process is not yet complete, and in many parts of the world it is far from being so. Its accomplishment in the shortest time possible is a priority for development, allowing the strengthening of human capital and at the same time helping to allow development to proceed in a balanced way. No less important is the fact that the incomplete transition is also reflected in serious inequalities between countries, groups, and individuals. It is essential that, in the coming decades, we concentrate on the interactive circuit that links the availability of food to nutrition, to the spread of avoidable diseases, to survival and reproductive behaviours, and therefore to demographic growth. This has aptly been defined as the Malthusian 'trap': the trap that ensnarls societies with high demographic growth. Suffering food shortages, diseases, and high mortality, they maintain high reproduction rates, which in turn cause a further rise in the population and seal a circuit of poverty:

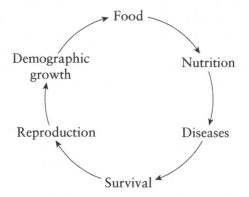

Two centuries ago this trap seemed to resist any attempt to elude it. However, contemporary society is capable of intervening to dismantle the trap by way of its incomparably more effective knowledge and resources. Yet this priority is drowned out amid the plethora of SDGs. I should thus pause to explain further the mechanisms that spring this trap and the actions capable of loosening its hold.

Let's begin with food. In future decades the predicted growth of the world's population and an increase in the economic means of famished or undernourished populations will cause a strong rise in food demand and considerable stress on the productive capacity of the world's agricultural system. Experts seem confident that this demand can be met through a moderate increase in the amount of land used for crops and a wise policy on water; but they also rely on a strong increase in productivity that should derive from new technologies and, most importantly, on the dissemination of the technology that already exists. The predictions of the Food and Agriculture Organization (FAO) indicate a rise in the world production of cereals from 2.3 billion tonnes in 2015 to 3 billion in 2050 (a 30 per cent rise) and a rise in meat production from 305 to 463 million tonnes (a 52 per cent rise) between those same two dates.[5] The production system will also have to provide for an improvement in nutrition levels in the countries where they are insufficient. Naturally this will place considerable stress on production, which will be thick with uncertainties about its environmental effects, also as a result of the possible further growth of demand for biofuels. Risks could also emerge from the climate change that results from global warming. The imperfect or distorted functioning of the markets, the persistence of major inequalities of income distribution, mistaken public policy interventions, and political instability are other potential factors that could have a serious influence on future prospects. However, the slowing of demographic growth should make it easier to satisfy the demand from poor populations than it was in the past.

While this gives us a global picture, it has to be broken down and reconstructed region by region, country by country, society by society, layer by layer in a world that remains deeply unequal. Table 8.1 presents the dietary energy supply (DES) index, which measures the average calories daily available to any individual (of any age and gender). These are mean values, useful for seeing the progress that has been achieved and the inequalities among large geographic areas. We will take a detailed look only at South Asia and sub-Saharan Africa, where the concentration of hungry people is six out of ten. Overall, the world did take some forward steps in the two decades in question and the calories available to the populations of the less developed countries increased by 15 per cent per capita, cutting the gap with the rich world. But the progress was rather weaker in the two subcontinents where the starting point was lower.

Table 8.1   Energy supply in various regions of the world, in 1990–92 and 2012–14 (per capita daily calories)

	1990–92	2012–14	change %
South Asia	2,292	2,487	+8.5
India	2,278	2,455	+7.8
Pakistan	2,297	2,451	+6.7
Sub-Saharan Africa	2,138	2,391	+11.8
Developing countries	2,413	2,769	+14.8
Developed countries	3,257	3,399	+4.4

Source: FAO, *Food Security Indicators* (at http://www.fao.org/economic/ess/ess-fs/ess-fadata/it/#.VXHkvNLtmko)

The FAO has designed another measure, called the 'average dietary energy supply adequacy' of each country (Table 8.2). It consists of the proportional relation between the average calorie supply and the population's actual needs. An index of around 100 means that food provision would only be sufficient in the (wholly theoretical) case of perfect equality of access among a country's citizens. But, since there is in fact grave inequality everywhere, an index of 100 would indicate a very high proportion of people who wake up hungry and go to bed still being hungry. Even countries with indexes of up to 115 are hit hard by the scourge of malnutrition.

Some progress was made in sub-Saharan Africa in the period between 1990–2 and 2012–14, where the adequacy index rose from 106 to 110 (see Table 8.2). In South Asia, the other large region at risk, there was rather more modest progress (from 106 to 109). China seems to have left the ghost of hunger definitively behind it (together with the ghost of the tens of millions who died from the famine of 1959–61), as the adequacy index has jumped from 106 to 127. In the developing countries taken as a whole there have been substantial steps forward. But it is worth noting that, even in countries that do have an adequate calorie consumption, there may nonetheless persist serious shortages of essential nutrients (iron, zinc, sodium, vitamins). Hence an adequate number of calories does not mean adequate nutrition.

Presented in summary, the tendencies of recent decades show both lights and shadows. Lights, because an ever more crowded world seems able, as a whole, to respond to the

Table 8.2   Index of the adequacy of energy supply, 1990–92 and 2012–14

	1990–92	2012–14	change %
South Asia	106	109	+2.8
India	105	108	+2.9
Pakistan	108	108	=
Sub-Saharan Africa	106	110	+3.8
Developing countries	108	119	+10.2
Developed countries	132	135	+2.3

Source: FAO, *Food Security Indicators* (at http://www.fao.org/economic/ess/ess-ts/ess-fadata/it/#.VXHkvNLtmko)

growing demand for food and because even cautious predictions give reason to hope that this will continue also in the decades to come. Shadows, because of the negative side effects that an intensified production has on the environment, market malfunction, the unknowns of climate change, and the increased frequency of 'food emergencies' that result from natural or man-made events. But the most worrying 'shadow' lies in the increase in inequalities between the different regions of the world and the persistence of situations of grave food inadequacy in the Indian subcontinent and in the countries to the south of the Sahara, as well as in other parts of the word (from Haiti to the Dominican Republic, Bolivia, Paraguay, Cambodia, Laos, and Myanmar). These are the populations most tightly in the grip of the Malthusian trap, and the countries where it is most difficult to loosen its hold.

The most troubling thing when we think about the masses of people who still today go hungry is the great vulnerability of young children. Good nutrition is a guarantee of the proper growth in both body and mind; it underpins and encourages the development of one's intellectual capacities and, ultimately, the formation of human capital. Insufficient nutrition weakens the immune system's defences and increases the risk of contracting infectious diseases. Studies in poor countries – in Africa and South Asia in particular – show that a considerable proportion of children under the age of 5 are underweight or display signs of wasting and stunted growth (or both). Wasting levels, among children under 5, of the order of 10–20 per cent (as in some of the countries listed in Table

8.3) can be compared to figures of under 5 per cent in the rest of the poor world (and around 2 per cent in China, Mexico, and Brazil). India is a paradoxical case: a large country, which is at the forefront of information technology, space activities, and atomic research yet remains far from solving its food problems. According to the latest sample study (from 2006), one in five children under 5 in India suffered from wasting, and almost a half were below average height. It also emerges from the data that there is no direct relation between infant mortality and the anthropometric measures to which we referred above: wasting, stunted growth, and being underweight do not necessarily lead to death, even if they do increase the risks (although the health system can do much to avoid this). They do, however, have a negative effect on children's physical and cognitive capacities, with consequences that extend across these individuals' entire lifespan.

Suffering hunger and its serious consequences is perhaps the worst aspect of backwardness, which entails many other ills – such as disease, the lack of the most basic hygiene,

Table 8.3 Percentage of children under 5 suffering from wasting, stunted growth, underweightness, and mortality per 1,000 children of this same age

	% wasting	% stunted growth	% underweight	mortality
Bangladesh (2011)	15.7	41.4	36.8	56
India (2006)	20.0	47.9	43.5	64
Pakistan (2011)	14.8	43.0	30.9	78
Ivory Coast (2007)	14.0	39.0	29.4	123
DR Congo (2010)	8.5	43.5	24.2	194
Ethiopia (2010)	10.1	44.2	29.2	92
Kenya (2009)	7.0	27.7	16.4	90
Nigeria (2011)	10.2	36.0	24.4	142

Sources: FAO, *Food Security Indicators* (at http://www.fao.org/economic/ess/ess-fs/ess-fadata/it/#.VXHkvNLtmko); United Nations, *World Population Prospects*: The 2012 Revision. New York, 2013 (at http://esa.un.org/unpd/wpp/unpp/panel_population.htm)
Note: Dates in brackets refer to the last available anthropometric study; infant mortality refers to the 2005–2010 period

precarious housing, adverse environmental conditions, the lack of education, and the absence of infrastructure and services. Increased survival rates, still so precarious in the poor countries – in 2010–15 sub-Saharan life expectancy stood at 53 years, the level attained in Italy in the late 1920, before the invention of antibiotics and sulpha drugs – pass for an overall improvement in living conditions. There are probably no specific interventions able to give the decisive impulse for change, also because the context varies from country to country. For instance, one might think that in sub-Saharan Africa substantial investment in water supplies would allow for a reduction of the very high proportion of the population (36 per cent) that lacks access to safe sources of drinking water, with imaginable consequences for the spread of infectious diseases. There are countries – like Cuba and Sri Lanka, for example – where poverty has not prevented very strong progress in survival rates. But there are also opposite cases.

The international community – and in the first place the World Health Organisation – has limited resources to intervene at the level of healthcare. However, there are examples of success with well-organised actions directed at achieving specific results. One example is the Global Fund to Fight AIDS, Tuberculosis and Malaria, founded in 2001 upon the initiative of the G8, under the umbrella of the United Nations. This public–private partnership (with considerable financial support from the Bill and Melissa Gates Foundation) today administers two thirds of the international funds for the fight against malaria and tuberculosis and a fifth of the funds for fighting AIDS. Naturally, it is rather difficult to separate out the effects of international action as distinct from those resulting from the mobilisation of states' own domestic resources. However, it certainly is true that in the last ten years or so these tremendous scourges have been contained and pushed back, achieving the sixth Millennium Development Goal ('Combat HIV/AIDS, Malaria and other diseases'). Between 2001 and 2012 the number of new cases of HIV infection was cut in half; in the same period mortality on account of malaria fell by 42 per cent, while mortality on account of tuberculosis was halved as compared to 1990.[6] Continuing to combat these and other diseases, as well as to eradicate them (and the latter is indeed possible), will require both human and financial resources. Experts estimate – with reference to 2014 figures – a deficit of 3 to 5 billion dollars for the resources needed to fight against AIDS, one of 2.4 billion for the campaign against malaria, and one of 2 billion for the battle against tuberculosis. Together this amounts to 7 to 9 billion dollars, equivalent to something between one third and a quarter of the world's arms exports in 2013 and around 5 to 7 per cent of the official development aid (ODA) dispensed by the rich countries in 2014. It is not out of place to note that the aggregate number of deaths due to these three causes is estimated at around 3 million per year – around 7 per cent of the annual deaths in the developing world and twice or three times more in the worst exposed African countries.

In societies where survival is precarious and infant mortality high, it is not easy to decouple reproductive behaviours from the biological and instinctual conditions that have governed them for millennia. As I have often repeated, the history of the modern demographic transition begins with declining mortality, which is followed, after a longer or shorter delay, according to the circumstances, by a fall in birth rates. Across a large part of Africa, in the face of backward but improving survival rates, fertility is still very high.[7] The recourse to methods of birth control, either traditional or modern, remains limited. The age at which people have their first sexual relations, their first union, and their first child is everywhere very low. Taking the continent as a whole, the average number of children per woman was over six in the 1990s, before falling to 5.1 by 2010–15 (Table 8.4). In some countries like Nigeria (the continent's most populous state), Niger, the two Congos, Mali, Somalia, and Chad women have six or more children – triple of what would be necessary to maintain a stationary population. In these countries voluntary birth control is almost non-existent. The situation is different in South Africa and the countries of North Africa, in most of which birth rates are between two and three children per woman. The persistence of high fertility rates urgently demands appropriate social policies, more education, the valorisation of women's work, and the introduction of welfare measures designed to free the older generations of complete dependency on transfers from their children. However, these are all measures that require a lot of time for

Table 8.4 Number of children per woman in Africa and the rest of the world, 1950–2015

	1950–5	1980–5	2010–15
North Africa	6.81	5.67	3.27
Sub-Saharan Africa	6.53	6.69	5.10
Africa	6.60	6.46	4.71
Less developed countries	6.08	4.18	2.65
Developed countries	2.83	1.84	1.67
World	4.97	3.60	2.51

Source: United Nations, *World Population Prospects: The 2012 Revision*. New York, 2013 (at http://esa.un.org/unpd/wpp/unpp/panel_population.htm)

their effects to play out. It is thus necessary to strengthen family planning programmes, which, if run well, can put powerful downward pressure on birth rates. In this regard it is worth citing the cases of Rwanda and Ethiopia, which have adopted vigorous programmes in the last decade, with the intention of spreading awareness of the advantages of more moderate reproduction levels. They also embarked on an intensive and territorially far-reaching effort to encourage access to contraception. In Rwanda the number of children per woman fell from 6.1 to 4.6 between 2005 and 2010; in Ethiopia (Africa's second most populous country) there was a smaller but still quite substantial fall from 5.4 to 4.8 children per woman between 2005 and 2011. Nonetheless, for the continent as a whole, recent trends are worrying. In Kenya, a country whose first family-planning programmes date back to the 1960s and where there was a substantial decline in birth rates up until the 1990s, a long period of stagnation followed. In recent years this has led the government to relaunch its family planning policies. The results are still to be measured. In other big countries such as Nigeria and the Democratic Republic of Congo, already mentioned above, there has been no change in reproductive models. An ambitious nationwide programme was adopted in Nigeria in 2004, but it had no effect on birth rates. Naturally, even where programmes and their objectives are ambitious, they are doomed to fail without a determined and active political commitment at all levels and without deployment of resources.

As we have already seen, a large share of the world population that lives in extreme poverty and hunger inhabits the big countries of the Indian subcontinent (India, Pakistan, and Bangladesh). However, these countries do have relatively solid institutions and governments, full awareness of the importance of demographic factors of development, and a higher social level. All this translates into a belated but now advanced demographic transition, even if the rate of population increase is still very high – currently around 1.3 per cent a year, half of what it is in sub-Saharan Africa. These are societies where a decisive relaxation of the suffocating Malthusian mechanism is close at hand – and coherent social policies could bring it closer still.

Poverty, shortages and insufficient nutrition, high disease rates, elevated mortality, uncontrolled reproduction and its corollary – too young mothers and precarious health for both mothers and infants: these are the classic links in the chain that suffocates development. Breaking them is, still today, a priority for the international community and, of course, for governments. Yet this is an international community that seems to consider the demographic question a matter of the past, or at least not a priority. As I have repeatedly emphasised, it is wrong to do so. There are three basic reasons why this matter should be put back at the centre of the debate. The first is that, while the trap can be dismantled, this will take coherent and decisive actions, including ones that follow the trail of policies experimented in the past. Hunger can be contained and defeated; the worst diseases can be resisted and survival rates improved; reproduction can be put under control. The resources exist, and so does the expertise. The second reason is that adequate nutrition, good health, and controlled reproduction are essential elements of human capital, decisive for development. The third is that weaknesses in terms of these structuring elements of human capital are one of the major causes of inequalities. Hunger and malnutrition compromise the balanced development of those who suffer from them, increase the risk of remaining in poverty, and are linked to fewer birth controls and a large number of children. Thus the Malthusian trap is reproduced at both the individual and the family level.

Epilogue

Our Shrinking Planet

- A thousand times more crowded, a thousand times smaller
- Still today a pendulum of fear between overpopulation and depopulation
- Seven demographic and political notes
- Awareness of limits

I said it already at the start: in 10,000 years of history the planet has got 1,000 times smaller – or, if you prefer, 1,000 times more crowded. Within a half-century, give or take a year, humanity will hit the 10 billion mark. There are two opposite philosophies for evaluating humanity's rapid numerical growth. The first tends to see it as an important phenomenon, certainly, but ultimately one that will have little influence on development, which is exercised by powerful endogenous social, political, and economic forces. The second, conversely, sees it as a dangerous path, one that feeds and aggravates the permanent conflict between population and resources. I have noted, moreover, that the pendulum of public opinion swings between fear of depopulation and fear of excessive growth. I do not subscribe to either philosophy, albeit not out of any love for some non-existent middle way. Rather out of recognition that humanity does have the capacity to regulate and adapt its own behaviours – including demographic ones – as circumstances change. These capacities were relatively constricted throughout much of human history, dominated as this history was by natural, biological, and instinctual mechanisms. However, they were liberated in the last two centuries with the unfolding of the demographic transition, which remains incomplete across large parts of the world.

These concluding pages are dedicated to two reflections. The first regards demographic growth in the current century and the policies that are necessary or desirable for regulating or modifying its path, and indeed for absorbing and attenuating its possible negative consequences. The second concerns what it will mean for humanity to live on a planet that, having lost its immensity, is now discovering its limits. A shrinking planet, to be precise.

During an exceptional twentieth century the world population quadrupled (from 1.6 to 6.1 billion). During the twenty-first century it will fall short of doubling, and experts consider it likely that the ultimate total will remain under 11 billion, with close to zero growth towards the end of this period. Even so, it is also true that the absolute increase in world population numbers during this century will be about the same as it was in the twentieth century. Some argue that the world is heading toward the 'end of demography' – that is, a stationary balance that will gradually include the various regions of the world and their populations. It is thought that the completion of the demographic transition and a global levelling out of the inequalities between countries will inevitably lead to a homogenisation of demographic behavours.

This hypothesis seems rather unrealistic, and for many various and obvious reasons. The first is that thus far globalisation has brought an increase and not a decrease in the inequalities between countries. Moreover, the demographic inequalities between countries are today at historical highs: there are populations that produce an average of six children per woman and others that produce barely one, populations with a life expectancy close to 90 and others at not even a half of that, countries with demographic exoduses of biblical proportions and countries that absorb these same exoduses. It would be difficult indeed for the demographic transition to wipe out these differences, just as it is unthinkable that there could be a worldwide economic and social 'levelling out'. In fact, even if this did take place, the force of inertia inherent in highly differentiated age structures – younger populations that have only recently reduced their fertility from earlier higher levels, and older ones that rise from low levels – would bring about powerful demographic cycles that would not be in synchrony across the countries and regions of the world. Ultimately we can presume that the capacities to adapt mentioned above would impress further cycles of growth or decrease on the world's population, even after the end of the twenty-first century. Geodemography – which feeds geopolitics – has undergone profound changes and will continue to undergo them across the rest of the century. The effects for the world order will be of the utmost importance: one need only think of the shrinking of Europe, of Africa's becoming a giant, and of the demographic weakening of China.

In this scenario we face an assortment of demographic questions and problems that will compromise development and its sustainability, the political order, and the relations between countries. These are problems that can be attenuated, if not resolved, through appropriate social policies implemented by governments with the support of the international community. I have repeatedly mentioned them, but it is worth summarising them again, in conclusion.

1   Low or very low reproduction rates in the majority of rich countries and in a growing number of poor countries, which are unsustainable in the long term: there are no simple recipes for a recovery in fertility rates. However, certain profound changes in welfare systems' distributive mechanisms, altered to the advantage of families with children, promise much in the long term. If not, only immigration can combat some of the negative aspects of the serious reproduction deficit.
2   Persistently high reproduction rates among over a billion people, which, together with moderate mortality, generate a demographic growth without parallels in world history: the experience of the last half-century shows that non-coercive family planning programmes, combined with suitable social policies, are able to moderate reproductive behaviours.

3   In South and East Asia, the powerful distortion of the relative numbers of each sex at birth: this is the result of a restrictive demographic policy (in the Chinese case), the persistent social devaluation of women, and technological innovations that allow for an advance diagnosis of the unborn child's sex. The implications are unsustainable and unacceptable at the level of values and negative on account of the distortions they cause to the normal gender structure of the population. This has a grave distorting effect on the mechanisms of couple and union formation.[1]

4   The 'Malthusian trap', out of which a major part of humanity is struggling to break, afflicted as it is by hunger, malnutrition, infectious diseases, and the lack of birth controls (point 2): this trap slows down or prevents development and feeds inequalities between countries and individuals.

5   The fact that breaking out of the 'Malthusian trap' implies a dangerous growth in the consumption of energy and non-renewable raw materials: as the parable of Tycoonia and Pauperia demonstrates, this has a heavy environmental impact. Birth-control policies can cushion the problem, while development and the transferral of new technologies can facilitate solutions to it.

6   The fact that space that has been directly or indirectly affected by human activity is growing, while free spaces are shrinking: states' and the international community's policies must get a grip on the disorder of human settlements, which is due to demographic growth in fragile environments, human intrusion into the rainforests, concentration along the coasts, and unruly urbanisation.

7   International migration, ungoverned and without rules: this happens thanks to states' refusal to cede even tiny fragments of their sovereignty in this regard, and thanks to the weakness of supranational institutions.

Evidently some of these seven points are closely interlinked, and many interventions and solutions will have a plural effect. In some cases the prescriptions are already tried and tested but the political will and the capacity – or the resources – to implement them are lacking. Such is the case with policies designed to reduce birth rates or to control the major transmissible diseases; and, within limits, the same is also true of the struggle against malnutrition. In other cases there is a total lack of political will; international migration, for instance, is one such case. In yet other cases the necessary interventions are possible but multiple and complex, requiring a well-structured plan and long-term policies that are sustained on an ongoing basis.

The international community is preparing to advance new watchwords on sustainable development, formulating a series of objectives for the next fifteen years. These are the sustainable development goals, which we criticised in Chapters 4 and 7 on two counts. One of the criticisms concerns a general point of method, the other a specific point of substance. The point of method: a range of 200-odd objectives (as they emerge from the draft in preparation for the UN summit) is a review or a list of the world's ills. However, such an exercise is useless for formulating strategies of intervention, which must recognise and be convinced about the priorities for action. It is also useless – if not damaging – in terms of mobilising awareness, energies, and resources. On the specific point of substance: even though this list is very long, demographic questions have either slipped away or been drowned out. Yet some of these questions constitute very serious obstacles to precisely the sustainable development that the goals are meant to encourage.

The second consideration concerns the consequences that the advent of a shrinking planet will have for human society. Obviously this is rather a simplification: such a development is gradual and its consequences may prove difficult to see. Even so, the crowding of the planet is taking place at a speed without historical precedent. It is worth us reflecting on the significance of this change. In the first place – as I said in the introduction – the perception is spreading that certain limits have been reached, or are being approached, or have become visible. Today more than half the world is anthropised, either directly or indirectly; the speed of communications has enormously shortened distances; the relative costs of moving people, the goods they produce, or the words they write or say have fallen. Crowding also means the intensification of contacts among people and the shrinking of empty spaces. The planet's physical limits are now visible and they continue to be effectively uncrossable. One interesting aspect, in this regard, is the slowdown – or, in some cases, arrest and reversal – of the growth of big megalopolises in the rich countries: cities that risk collapsing under the weight of their own population. One might also reflect on the fact that many of the countries with weak or declining population growth also have very high population density (Japan, China, South Korea, Germany, Italy). Naturally there are also interesting counterexamples (for instance Russia), but here we are talking about social phenomena, which are not governed by mechanical laws.

Then there are other limits, of a more properly demographic character. Certainly there is a limit to the duration of human life and, judging by the slowdown in the extension of lifespans, this is a limit that we are now approaching. We have reached the minimum limit of low birth rates – in some countries this comes close to one child per woman, the minimal empirical point in reproduction rates in any advanced society. There is a strengthening of the limits that migration policies pose to international flows of people, and in a growing number of cases they are concretised as insuperable physical barriers.

In an ever smaller and more crowded planet, both pessimists and optimists will find material to back up their own convictions. The first can fear that competition and conflicts will become sharper or that new barriers and fresh segregation will emerge if such consequences are to be avoided. The second are confident that the intensification of human relations – whether those driven by migration and mobility or those mediated by ever denser and more integrated communications – will lead to the kind of fourth globalisation to which we referred in Chapter 4: an economic globalisation, but also a human and social one, with positive effects for global relations. I like to think that the world might head in this direction.

Notes

Notes to Chapter 1

1 That is, women who did not die before the end of their fertile age.

2 I have based my estimates of the pre-1950 world population on three sources: Jean-Noël Biraben, 'Essai sur l'évolution du nombre des hommes', *Population* 34, 1979; Colin McEvedy and Richard Jones, *Atlas of World Population History*, Harmondsworth: Penguin Books, 1978; and Angus Maddison, *The World Economy: Historical Statistics*, Paris: OECD, 2003.

3 Estimates of the demographic 'weight' – and hence of the population – of the various continents were a matter of conjecture until the nineteenth century and should be considered as largely illustrative. For more details, see the works referred to in the previous note: Biraben, 'Essai', McEvedy and Jones, *Atlas*, and Maddison, *World Economy*.

4 In the Malthusian model, uncontrolled growth sets in motion high mortality as a destructive rebalancing mechanism. This can be avoided when populations apply 'pre-emptive brakes' that reduce the number of births, such as a rise in the age of marriage or celibacy.

5 It is rather difficult to identify the 'end' of the transition. But a fertility rate of 2.5 children per woman and a 70-year life expectancy are levels signalling that a population has 'entered' the terrain of moderate demographic growth, which I here consider to be an indicator of the end of the transition.

6 Well-designed social policies that strengthen women's education and autonomy, support the elderly and spread birth-control practices can have the effect of accelerating the fall in birth rates, thus doing much to contain the extent of demographic growth. I will return to these themes in Chapter 4.

Notes to Chapter 2

1 This is a simple multiplicative model.
2 Assuming that there are 2,500 calories per kilogram and that the 'average person' eats only cereal products.
3 Roger LeB. Hooke, José F. Martín-Duque, and Javier Pedraza, 'Land Transformation by Humans: A Review', *GSA Today* 22.12 (2012): 4–10.
4 Stephen G. Perez, Carlos Aramburu, and Jason Bremner, 'Population, Land Use and Deforestation in the Pan Amazon Basin', *Environment, Development and Sustainability* 7 (2005): 23–49.
5 Gordon McGranahan, Deborah Balk, and Bridget Anderson, 'The Rising Tide: Assessing the Risks of Climate Change and Human Settlements in Low Elevation Coastal Zones', *Environment & Urbanization* 19.1 (2007): 17–37.
6 It is worth adding that the concentration of people in urban areas is very strong in these same low-altitude coastal regions.
7 The following considerations are drawn from Massimo Livi Bacci, 'Popolazione ed energia', in *Economia ed Energia: Secoli XIII–XVIII: Atti della XXXIV settimana di studi dell'Istituto Internazionale di Storia Economica F. Datini (Prato, 15–19 aprile 2002)*, edited by Simonetta Cavaciocchi. Florence: Le Monnier, 2003, pp. 101–29.
8 International Panel on Climate Change, 2014 (text available at https://www.ipcc.ch/news_and_events/docs/ar5/ar5_syr_headlines_en.pdf).
9 John Graunt, 'Natural and Political Observations Made upon the Bills of Mortality' (text available at http://www.neonatology.org/pdf/graunt.pdf).
10 In this same period the middle-income countries contributed 36% of demographic growth and 53% of the rise in emissions.
11 International Panel on Climate Change (IPCC), *Climate Change, 2014: Synthesis Report, Summary for Policymakers* (available at https://www.ipcc.ch/pdf/assessment-report/ar5/syr/AR5_SYR_FINAL_SPM.pdf).

Notes to Chapter 3

1 On these examples, see Massimo Livi Bacci, *A Concise History of World Population*, 5th edn, Oxford: Wiley Blackwell, 2014, Ch. 2.

2 Women in hunter-gatherer groups would have had a moderated fertility, more functional to their continual movements. This would have been achieved by abating their sexual relations or by lengthening the periods of nursing. Some scholars deny that nutrition levels improved as humans settled on the land; on the contrary, they would have been weakened by diets that contained more cereal products and fewer animal proteins. The debate is still open.

3 Data drawn from United Nations, *World Fertility Report 2013: Fertility at the Extremes*, New York, 2013 (available at http://www.un.org/en/development/desa/population/publications/pdf/fertility/worldFertilityReport2013.pdf).

4 To tell the truth, even such a large country as Argentina had relatively low fertility in 1950–5 (3.2 children per woman). The 'rule of 5' is only a general orientation: in many of the countries indicated above where the number of children per woman reaches 5 or more, there is also a significant proportion of women and couples who practise some form of birth control. It is also worth mentioning that, even in contexts where fertility is very high, we can assume that a proporition of couples, even if small, use some means of avoiding pregnancy.

5 United Nations, Population Division, *World Abortion Policies*, 2013 (available at http://www.un.org/en/development/desa/population/publications/ policy/world-abortion-policies-2013.shtml).

6 The migrant 'stock' in each country is calculated on the basis of census data and refers to those counted who were born outside the country or, alternatively, to people of foreign nationality. See United Nations, Population Division, *International Migration Report*, 2013 (at http://www.un.org/en/development/desa/population/publications/pdf/migration/migrationreport2013/Full_Document_final.pdf). For the data, see Chapter 6 here.

7 This argumentation involves a certain logical stretch. When we speak of migration here, we mean the net balance of migration, namely the difference between immigrants and emigrants. The figures thus refer to a balance, not to real individuals who enter or leave. There would be no such strain if the positive balance meant only immigrants and zero emigrants.

8 On the famines of the last century, see Cormac Ó Gráda, *Famine: A Short History*, Princeton: Princeton University Press, 2006.

9 Associazione italiana per lo studio della popolazione (AISP), *Rapporto sulla popolazione: L'Italia nella crisi economica*, Bologna: Il Mulino, 2015.

Notes to Chapter 4

1 Quoted by Joel E. Cohen, *How Many People Can the Earth Support?* New York: Norton, 1995, p. 6.
2 The Brundtland Report [*translator's note:* the full title is *Report of the World Commission on Environment and Development: Our Common Future*] is named after the Norwegian president of the commission that authored it, Gro Harlemn Brundtland. It is available at http://www.un-documents.net/our-common-future.pdf.
3 One problem is that of time: Which future generations should we hold ourselves to be responsible to? How should we judge those actions that, in spite of having a negative impact on the environment, permit a more rapid and balanced growth afterwards, which the generations to come will be able to enjoy?
4 United Nations, *Report of the International Conference on Population and Development, Cairo, 5–13 September 1994*, New York, 1995 (at https://www.unfpa.org/sites/default/files/event-pdf/icpd_eng_2.pdf).
5 Three of the millennium development goals concerned infant mortality, reproductive health, and HIV/AIDS and other serious social diseases. The other five concerned the reduction of hunger and extreme poverty, education, gender equality, environmental sustainability, and a global partnership for development.
6 United Nations, *The Millennium Development Goals Report, 2015*, New York, 2015 (at http://www.un.org/millennium-goals/2015_MDG_Report/pdf/MDG%202015%20rev%20 (July%201).pdf).
7 United Nations, *A New Global Partnership: Eradicate Poverty and Transform Economies through Sustainable Development: The Report of the High-Level Panel of Eminent Persons on the Post-2015 Development Agenda*, 2013 (at http://www.un.org/en/development/desa/policy/untaskteam_undf/HLP%20P2015%20Report.pdf).
8 The 2015 revision corrected the earlier 2012 forecasts, which hypothesised that net migration flows between countries would fall to zero by 2100. See United Nations, *World Population Prospects: The 2012 Revision*, New York, 2013 (at http://esa.un.org/unpd/wpp/unpp/panel_population.htm).

9 Its absolute unsustainability also resides in the fact that, even if behaviours were to change radically, as if by miracle in 2051, the two populations would continue for a long time, by inertia, one to decline and the other to increase.

10 It is worth adding that the hypothesis of constant fertility suggested by this projection is coupled with a continuation of current tendencies in migration: thus Germany's demographic decline will continue notwithstanding a considerable injection of migrants, namely a net inward migration of almost 150,000 a year across the 35 years in question. Nigeria, conversely, will have a negative balance of 60,000 a year, which will be of little influence, given the country's demographic dimensions.

11 United Nations, *Framework of Actions for the Follow-Up to the Programme of Action of the International Conference on Population and Development (ICPD) beyond 2014*, Report of the Secretary-General, 2013, § 75 (at https://www.unfpa.org/sites/default/files/event-pdf/sg_report_on_icpd_operational_review_final.unedited.pdf).

12 It is calculated that a child costs around one quarter of family income.

13 Generally young men's and women's average expectation in terms of their desired or ideal number of children is around two.

14 United Nations, *A New Global Partnership: Eradicate Poverty and Transform Economies through Sustainable Development: The Report of the High-Level Panel of Eminent Persons on the Post-2015 Development Agenda*, 2013, § 75 (http://www.post2015hlp.org/wp-content/uploads/2013/05/UN-Report.pdf).

15 Sustainable Development Solutions Network (SDSN), *An Action Agenda for Sustainable Development*, June 2013 (http://unsdsn.org/wp-content/uploads/2013/06/140505-An-Action-Agenda-for-Sustainable-Development.pdf).

16 Here I am using the simple but effective formula proposed by Paul Ehrlich, according to which the environmental impact (I) of human activity is equal to the population number (P) multiplied by its economic means or affluence (A: associated with its capita real income) and by a technological coefficient (T). The greater the use of technology per unit of product, the smaller the quota of non-renewable resources and energy employed. Hence the formula $I = P \times A \times T$.

17 United Nations Environment Programme (UNEP), *Decoupling Natural Resource Use and Environmental Impacts from Economic Growth: A Report of the Working Group on Decoupling to the International Resource Panel*, 2011 (available at https://sustainabledevelopment.un.org/index.php?page=view&type=400&nr=151&menu=1515).

Notes to Chapter 5

1 Benito Mussolini, *Il discorso dell'Ascensione*, Rome: Libreria del Littorio, 1927, p. 17. He continued: 'Let's say it clearly. What are 40 million Italians faced with 90 million Germans and 200 million Slavs? Let's turn to the West: What are 40 million Italians faced with 40 million Frenchmen, plus the 90 million inhabitants of their colonies, or faced with 46 million Englishmen, plus the 450 million in their colonies? Gentlemen, if Italy is to count for something, it must appear at the threshold of the second half of this century with a population of no fewer than 60 million inhabitants.'
2 Friedrich Ratzel, *Politische Geographie*, Munich: Verlag von R. Oldenburg, 1897.
3 Cited by J. Spengler, *France Faces Depopulation*, Durham, NC: Duke University Press, 1938, vol. 1, p. 123.
4 Frank W. Notestein, 'Population and Power in Postwar Europe', *Foreign Affairs* 22.3 (1944): 389–403, at p. 389 (available on subscription at https://www.foreignaffairs.com/articles/western-europe/1944-04-01/population-and-power-postwar-europe).
5 Massimo Livi Bacci, 'Il futuro delle popolazioni islamiche in Europa', *Neodemos*, 12 January 2015 (at http://www.neodemos. info/il-futuro-delle-popolazioni-islamiche-in-europa-2); Pew Forum on Religion and Public Life, *The Future of the Global Muslim Population*, 15 January 2011 (at http://www.pewforum.org/interactives/muslim-population-graphic).
6 Following the so-called 'three fifths compromise' of 1787, the representation of the states in Congress and their tax burden were calculated on the basis of their free population plus three fifths of the number of 'unfree' residents (slaves), who did not have the right to vote.
7 The GDP of the world's leading countries in 2050 has been estimated on the basis of a growth model based on projections of their workforce, investment, technological changes, and level of human capital. The ranking of the top ten countries changes significantly (by comparison to 2014), China replacing the USA in first place, India rising from ninth to third place, and Germany falling from fourth to tenth. France, the United Kingdom, and Italy fall out of the top ten in favour of Indonesia, Mexico, and Nigeria – demographically vibrant countries with good growth prospects. See *The World in 2050: Will the Shift in Global Economic Power Continue?* Pricewaterhouse Coopers, February 2015 (at www.pwc. co.uk/economics).

8 These columns are the Composite Index of National Capability (CINC), the National Power Index (NPI), the Global Firepower Index (GFP), the National Security Index (NSI) and the Comprehensive National Power (CNP). The GFP places great weight on conventional military means and on military spending and aims above all at weighing up the (non-nuclear) strength of two states in conflict, whereas the NSI (developed by an Indian institute) is essentially concerned with security in the face of aggression, attributing particular importance to energy security (note the high ranking of a small country like Norway). The CINC, the NPI, and the CNP (all of which are developed in China and are chronologically uncertain) measure not only the countries' military capacity but also their general degree of political, social, and economic influence, using a range of indicators.
9 W. Lutz, W. P. Butz, and S. KC (eds.), *World Population and Human Capital in the Twenty-First Century*, Oxford: Oxford University Press, 2014.

Notes to Chapter 6

1 Martin Luís Guzmán, *El aguila y la serpiente*, Mexico City: Compañia General de Ediciones, 1956, p. 174.
2 Translator's note: The current US administration plans to extend the barrier along the entire length of the frontier.
3 International Organization of Migration (IOM), *Fatal Journeys*, Geneva: IOM, 2014, p. 11 (at https://publications.iom.int/system/files/pdf/fataljourneys_countingtheuncounted.pdf).
4 Also of some relevance to this argument is the change in the organisation of the world's states over the past two centuries. Around 1850 there were 169 sovereign states worldwide; the birth of big unitary states in Europe and of colonial empires reduced this number to 78 in 1900 and to 74 in 1950. Decolonisation brought the numbers up to 107 in 1960 and to 180 in 1980; by 2015 there were 215 (not least because of the disintegration of the Soviet Union and Yugoslavia). These processes of fragmentation and reconstruction are often ignored in writings on geopolitics (visit http://en.wikipedia.org/wiki/Lists_of_sovereign_states_by_year).
5 According to 2012 UN predictions, by 2095–2100 all countries worldwide will have net migration balances of close to zero. This is an extreme hypothesis, softened in the 2015 forecasts (see note 8 of Chapter 4).
6 Naturally, this is no automatic process: the empty spaces in the rich world are not destined to be filled by the surplus population in

the poor world. However, there will continue to be potential demographic pressure.

7 Branko Milanovic, *Global Income Inequality by the Numbers: In History and Now* (Policy Research Working Paper, n. 6259), World Bank, 2012, p. 27 (at http://documents.worldbank.org/curated/en/959251468176687085/pdf/wps6259.pdf).

8 John K. Galbraith, *The Nature of Mass Poverty*, Cambridge, MA: Harvard University Press, 1979.

9 The 'international dollar' (or Geary–Khamis dollar, from the name of the statisticians who suggested it) is a monetary unit conventionally used in comparing measures of different countries' economic importance. Pro capita income (GDP) is expressed in dollars adjusted for purchasing power parity, i.e. by taking account of the different price of equivalent goods in different countries (this generally means that they are less expensive in poorer countries than in richer ones).

10 However, this has negative effects on the countries of emigration, as they lose precious human capital necessary for their own development.

11 Angus Maddison, *Monitoring the World Economy, 1820–1992*, Paris: OECD, 1995, p. 61.

12 Kevin H. O'Rourke and Jeffrey G. Williamson, *Globalization and History: The Evolution of a Nineteenth-Century Atlantic Economy*, Cambridge, MA: MIT Press, 1999.

13 In the internationally used terminology, 'circular migration' is generally high-skilled migration, limited to a few years, with a view to the migrant's ultimate return to her country of origin in order to avoid depriving it of human capital. The country of origin is compensated 'with interest' by the migrant's return home with increased knowledges (and corresponding savings).

14 Berta Ares Queija, 'Mestizos, mulatos, zambaigos (Virreinato del Perú, siglo XVI)', in *Negros, Mulatos, Zambaigos*, edited by Ares Queija Berta and Alessandro Stella, Sevilla, Escuela de Estudios Hispano-Americanos, 2000, pp. 75–88.

15 Giampaolo Lanzieri, 'Towards an Annual Measure of Prevalence for Intermarriages in European Countries', paper presented at the European Population Conference, Stockholm, 13–16 June 2012.

16 World Tourism Organization (UNWTO), *Tourism Highlights*, 2014 (at http://dtxtq4w60xqpw.cloudfront.net/sites/all/files/pdf/unwto_highlights14_en.pdf).

17 *Digital, Social and Mobile*, 2015 (at https://www.slideshare.net/wearesocialsg/digital-social-mobile-in-2015).

18 Graeme Hugo, *The Changing Dynamics of the Australia/Asia Pacific Migration System* (Working Paper for the Department of Immigration and Citizenship), University of Adelaide, Department

of Immigration and Citizenship, 2011 (at https://www.border.gov.au/ReportsandPublications/Documents/research/changing-dynamics-migration-system.pdf).

Notes to Chapter 7

1 Thomas Hobbes, *Leviathan*, 13.9.

2 In 2014 it was 87 for women in Japan and 86 for women in the Italian regions of Trentino-Alto Adige, Veneto, Marche, and Umbria.

3 In this chapter I make wide use of data on mortality (or survival) rates generally drawn from tables of mortality. These data are drawn mostly from the Human Mortality Database, available online at http://www.mortality.org, as well as from the UN database at http://esa.un.org/wpp/Excel-Data/mortality.htm. The Italian data are also available at the Istat site, at http://demo.istat.it/unitav2012/index.

4 J. Oeppen and J. Vaupel, 'Broken Limits for Life Expectancy', *Science* 296.5570 (2002, 10 May): 1029–31. For Louis Dublin in 1928 the limit was 65 years (a level New Zealand had already surpassed even at the time); in 1951 Jean Bourgeois-Pichat set the limit at 76 for men and 78 for women (levels reached by Italian women in 1982 and by Italian men in 1999). For Jay Olshansky in 1999 the limit was 85 (reached by Italian women in 2013 and by Japanese women in 2002).

5 For example, in Japan the life expectancy upon reaching 100 has remained stable at 2.5 years for women and 2.2 years for men ever since 2001 (as of 2012).

6 In practice this means an annual increase of 0.16 years over the 2013–50 period and 0.1 years from 2050 to 2100, as against an annual increase of 0.29 years between 1963 and 2013.

7 As mentioned in the text, the comparativist arguments developed in these pages around the 100-year society and around societies with different lifespans are based on a stationary model. This model has another important characteristic, beyond the ones already indicated (births equalling deaths and zero rate of increase; constant age structure) – namely that the rates of birth and mortality (B/P and D/P) are reciprocally related to life expectancy. If life expectancy is 100 years, then these rates must each be equal to 1/100, i.e. 10 per 1,000 per year; if life expectancy is 40, then they must be 1/40, i.e. 25 per 1,000 per year. In reality, the age structure of the population of the '100-year society' could assume a variety of connotations, as differences from our presupposed stationary society would depend not only on migration (here supposed to be zero)

but also on fertility levels. Presupposing a stationary society implies that each generation reproduces itself, and thus that each woman brings at least one daughter into the world during her lifetime, with a total fertility rate equivalent to 2.07 (more boys than girls are born, and we also have to take into account the light degree of mortality that would affect the population before its members reach the end of reproductive life, even in the 100-year society). In Italy today the fertility rate is around 1.4 children per woman, around a third below the replacement fertility rate. The 100-year society would be different from what is projected here if fertility rates were above or below 2.07, or even if they strongly oscillated around that level.

8 For example, since the transmission of inheritance upon the parents' death will take place at an ever more advanced stage in their children's lives, other means for transferring resources will be found while they are still alive.

Notes to Chapter 8

1 Translator's note: text sourced from United Nations, 'Following up on Measures to Achieve the Millennium Development Goals' (at http://www.un.org/ga/president/62/issues/mdgs.shtml).

2 Information on the 25–7 September 2015 summit and the New York General Assembly's preparatory work can be found at https://sustainabledevelopment.un.org/post2015/summit.

3 United Nations, *Technical Report by the Bureau of the United Nations Statistical Commission (UNSC) on the Process of the Development of an Indicator Framework for the Goals and Targets of the Post-2015 Development Agenda* (available at https://sustainabledevelopment.un.org/content/documents/6754Technical%20report%20of%20the%20UNSC%20Bureau%20%20%28final%29.pdf).

4 A revision of the indicators is now under way, and they have been reduced to 230 in number. In the new list the two indicators mentioned above have been eliminated, but in the new list we find the acrobatic indicator 4.7.1 – 'Extent to which (i) global citizenship education and (ii) education for sustainable development, including gender equality and human rights, are mainstreamed at all levels in: (a) national education policies, (b) curricula, (c) teacher education and (d) student assessment' – and the equally acrobatic indicator 17.16.1 – 'Number of countries reporting progress in multi-stakeholder development effectiveness monitoring frameworks that support the achievement of the sustainable development goals' (visit

http://unstats.un.org/sdgs/indicators/Official%20List%20of%20
Proposed%20SDG%20Indicators.pdf).
5 Piero Conforti (ed.), *Looking Ahead in World Food and Agriculture: Perspectives to 2050*, Rome: FAO, 2011; Nikos Alexandratos and Jelle Bruinsma, *World Agriculture towards 2030/2050: The 2012 Revision*, FAO, ESA Working Paper 12-03, June 2012 (at http://www.fao.org/fileadmin/templates/esa/Global_persepctives/world_ag_2030_50_2012_rev.pdf). The mass spread of GM will probably allow a still greater increase in the production of cereals and other products.
6 United Nations, *The Millennium Development Goals Report, 2015*, New York, 2015 (at http://www.un.org/millenniumgoals/2015_MDG_Report/pdf/MDG%202015%20rev%20(July%201).pdf).
7 The demographic and health surveys and the relevant national dossiers available at http://dhsprogram.com/data are of immense value to our knowledge of Africa's population.

Note to Epilogue

1 I did not deal explicitly with this argument in the previous chapters, where I gave priority instead to themes regarding sustainable development. The gradual alteration of the natural numbers of newborn boys relative to girls – hovering around 1.05 to 1.07 males to 1 female – was apparent in China from the 1980s onward, in parallel with the introduction of the one-child policy in a society with traditional preferences for male children. The ease of determining the newborn's sex in advance and simple recourse to selective abortion have brought a gradual increase in this disparity, which reached a ratio of 1.17 males to females (in 2005–10) and over 1.20 in various populous provinces. However, major alterations in the ratio between the sexes have also taken place among populations not restricted by rigid policies: in South Korea this same ratio rose to 1.14 in the 1990s and afterwards returned gradually to normal levels; in India it rose to 1.11 (in 2005–9), and was even over 1.2 in certain areas (Delhi, Haryana); in Vietnam, to 1.10; in Pakistan, to 1.09; in Caucasia, to 1.17 in Muslim Azerbaijan and to 1.15 in Christian Armenia. Selective abortion does indeed generate distortions in the 'marriage market' but most of all mirrors troubling cultural preferences.

Index